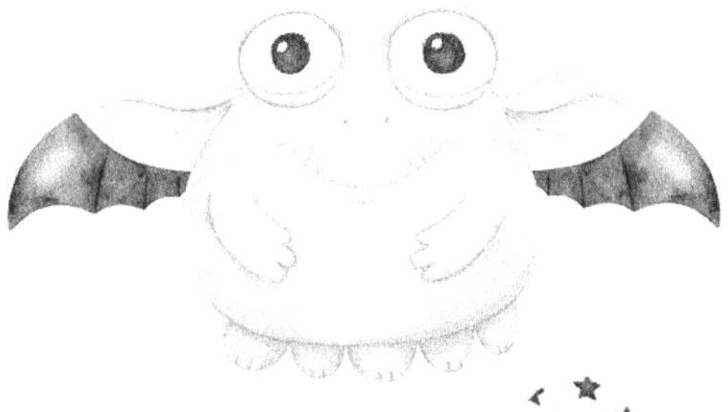

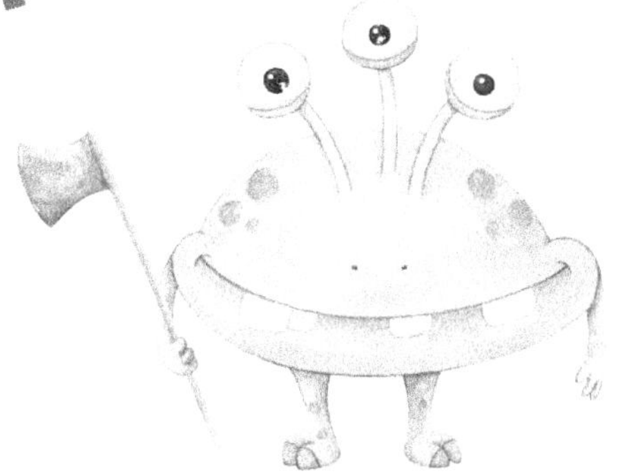

MY FIRST BIG BOOK OF MONSTERS

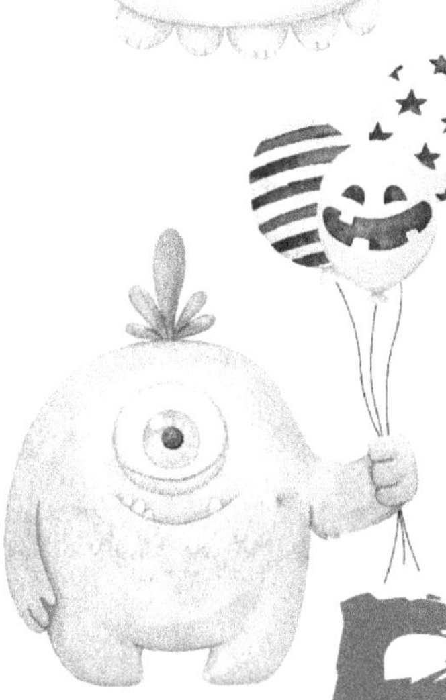

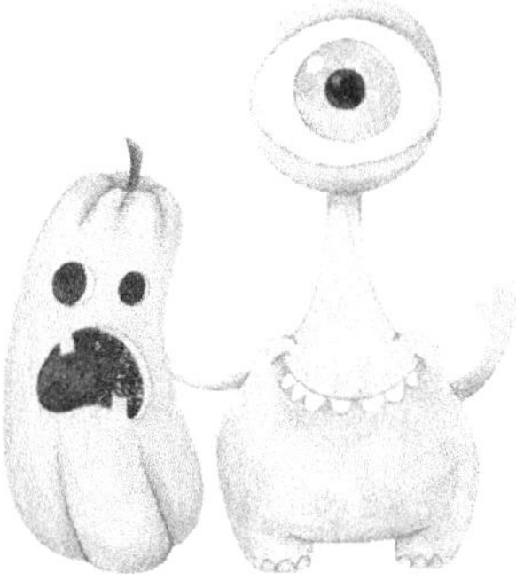

MY FIRST BIG BOOK OF COLORING

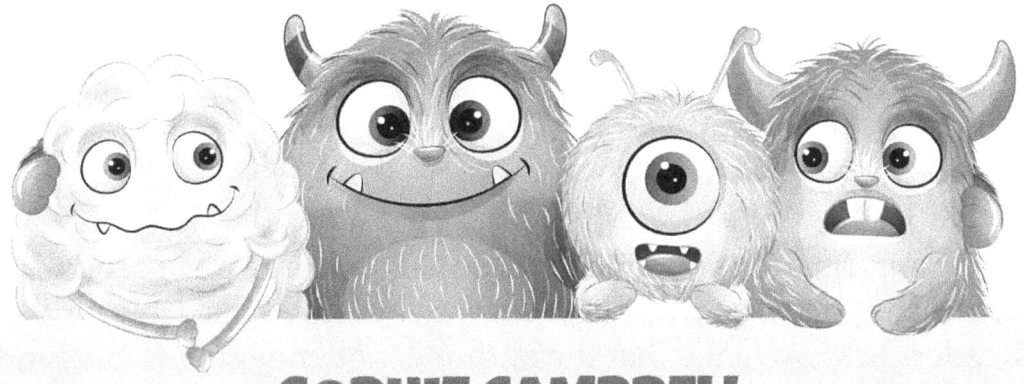

SOPHIE CAMPBELL

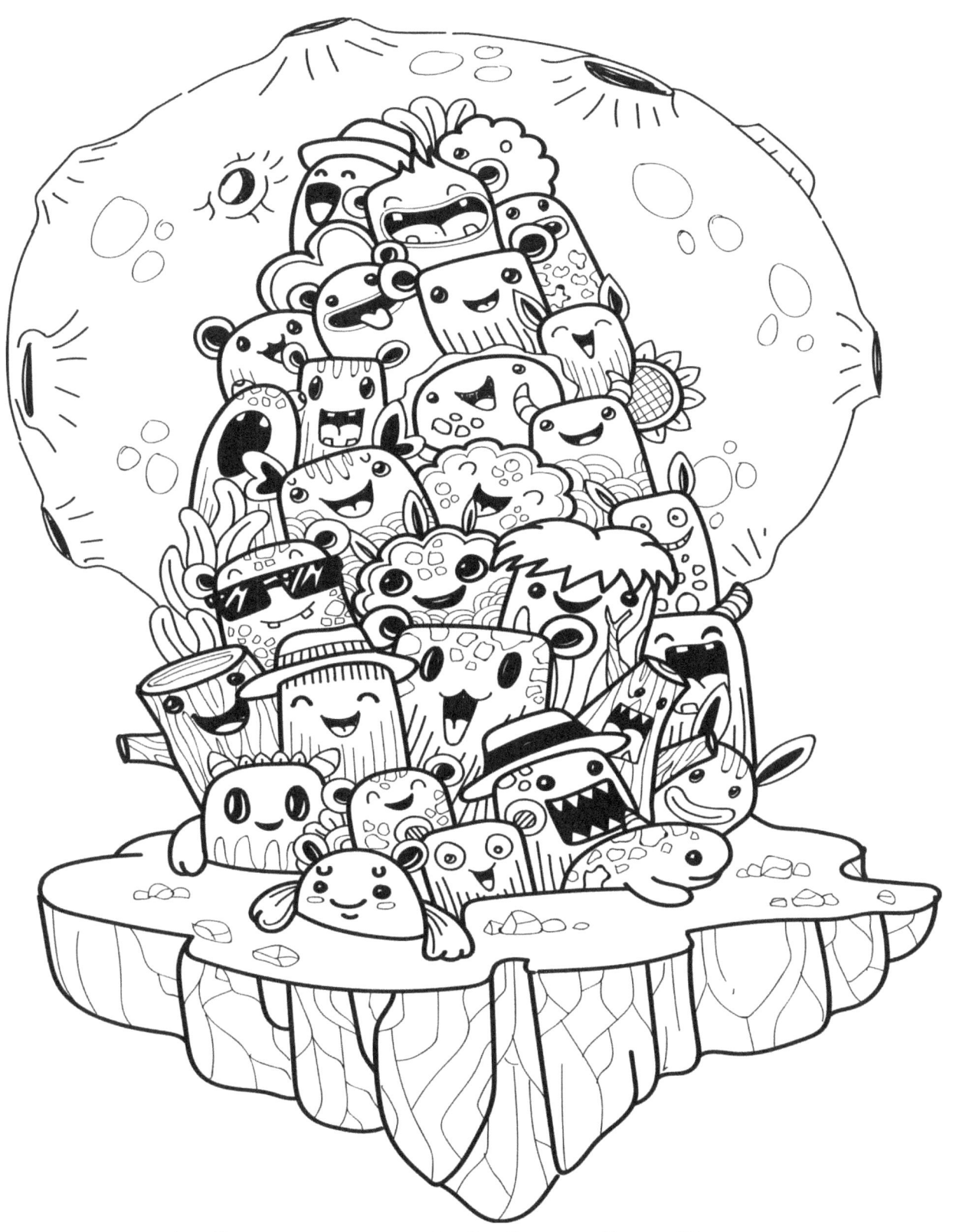

THIS BOOK BELONGS TO:

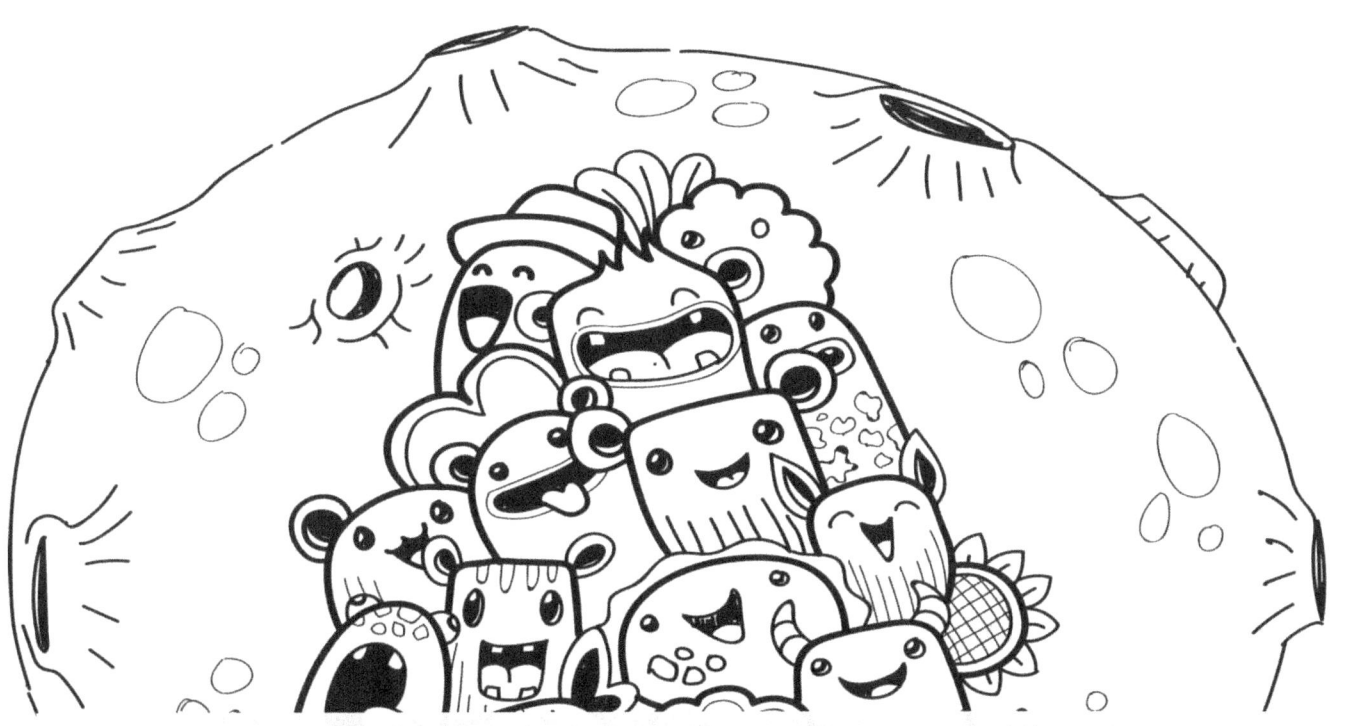

HERE YOU'LL FIND AND COLOR THE CUTEST AND SCARY MONSTERS. YOU CAN ALSO CUT THE PAGES AND COLOR THEM EASILY. GET FUN!

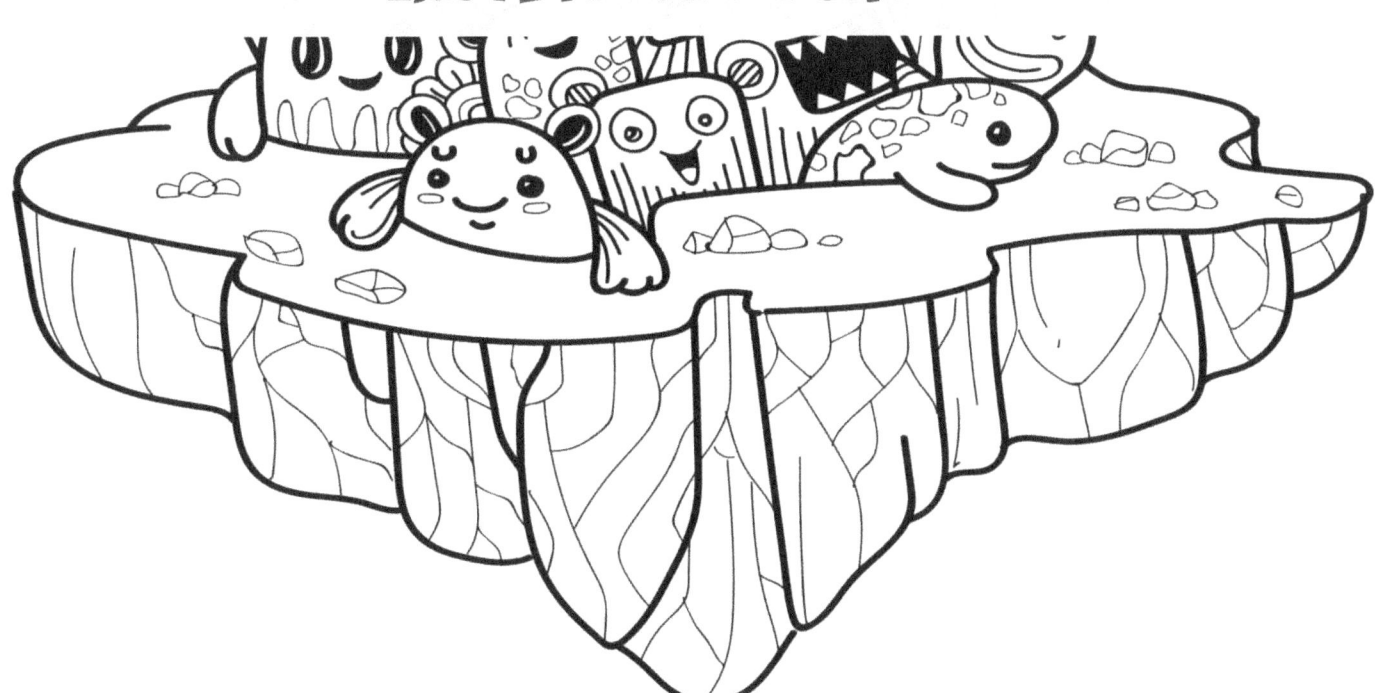

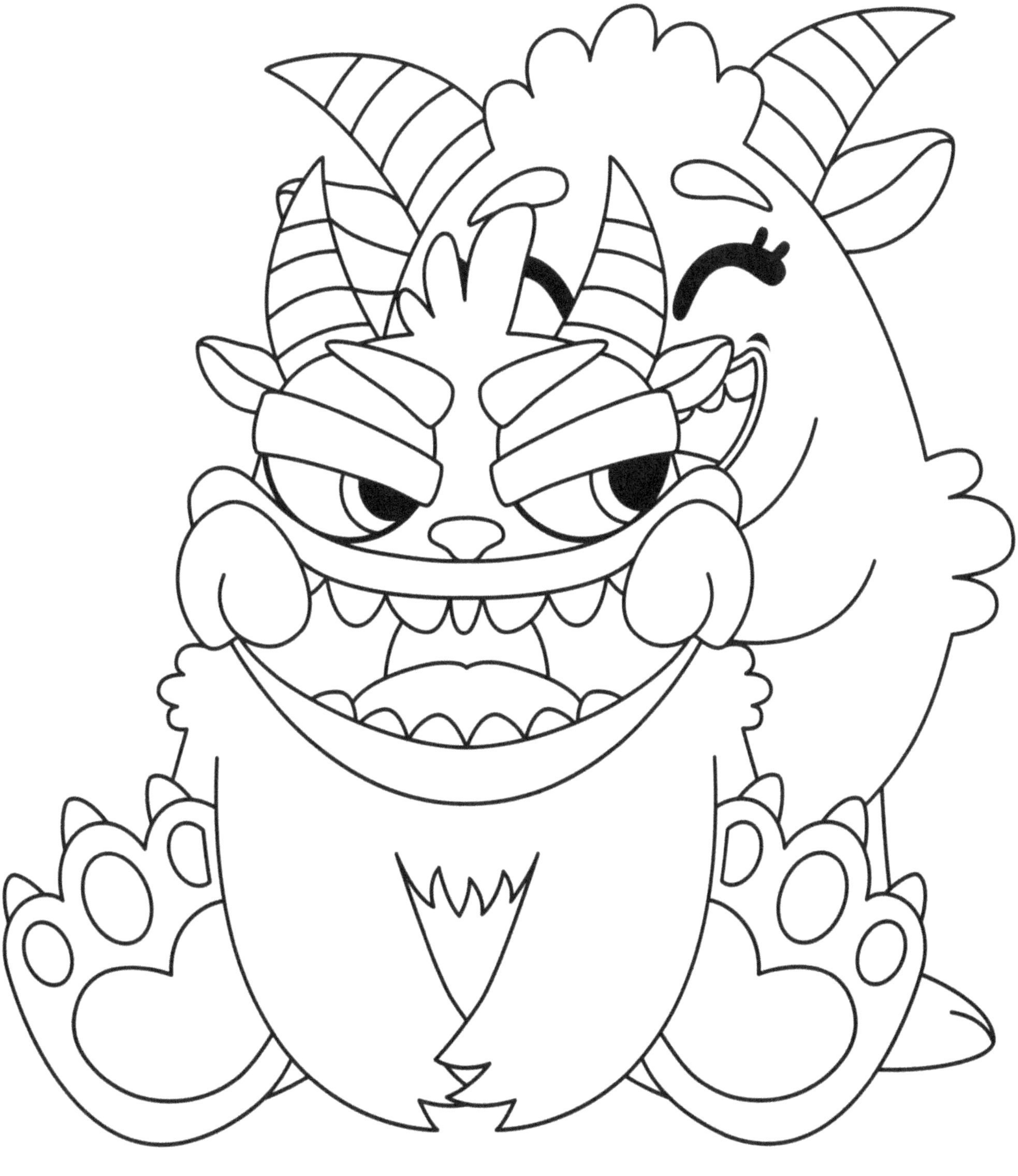

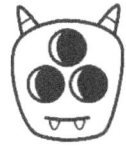
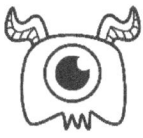

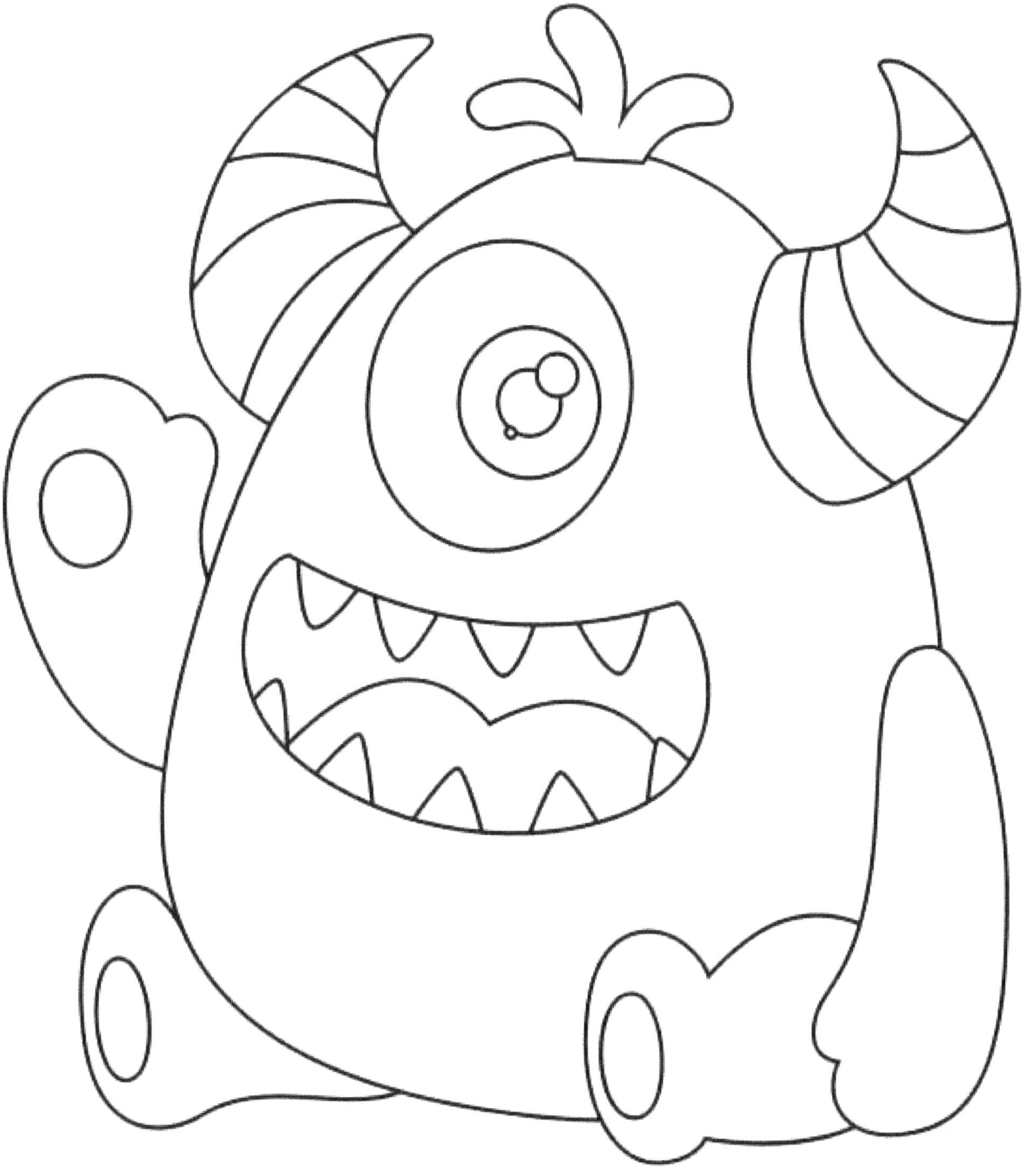

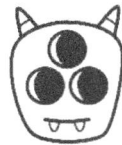
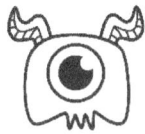

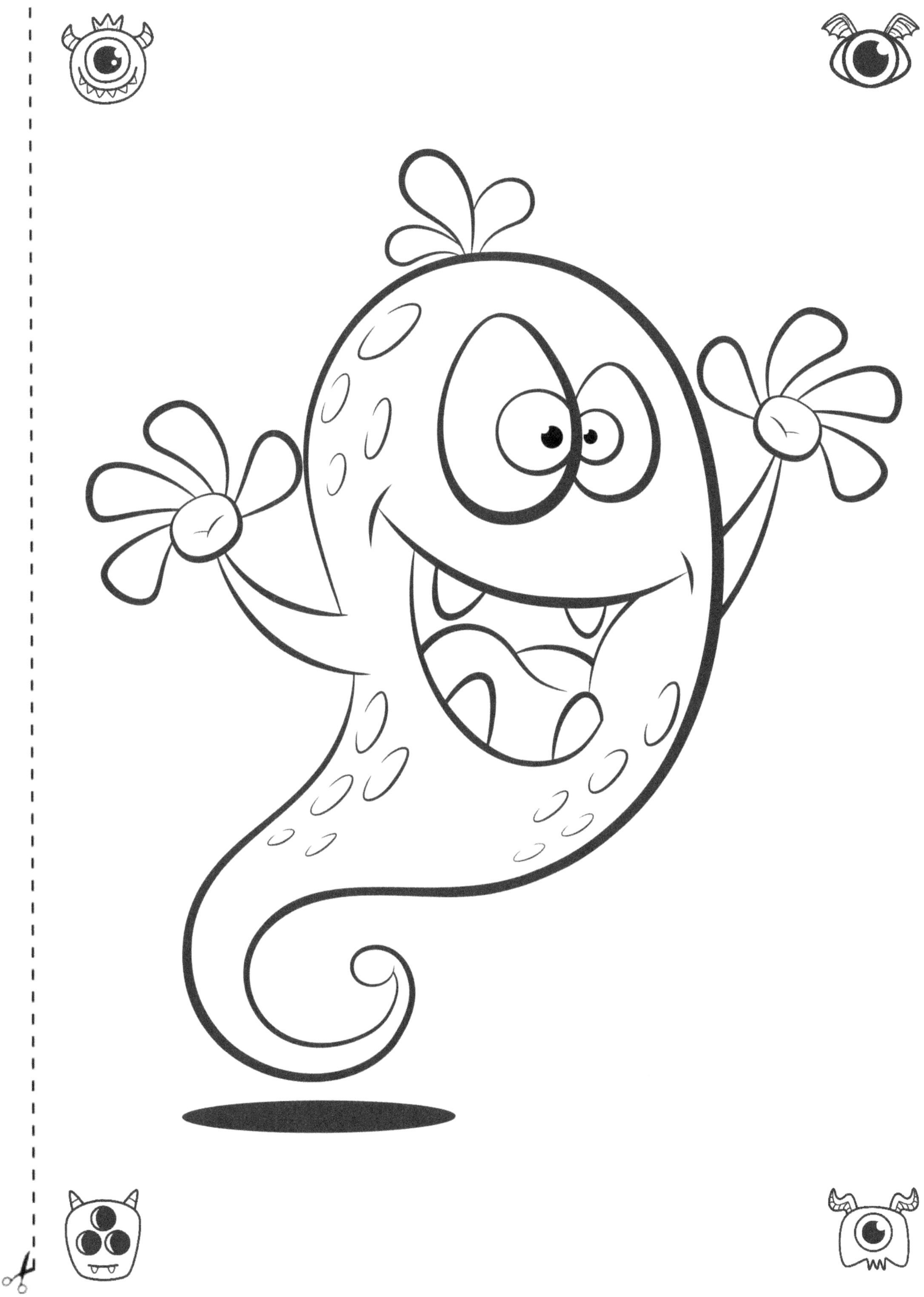

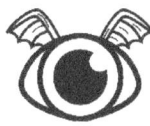
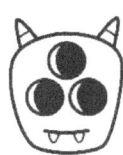
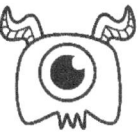

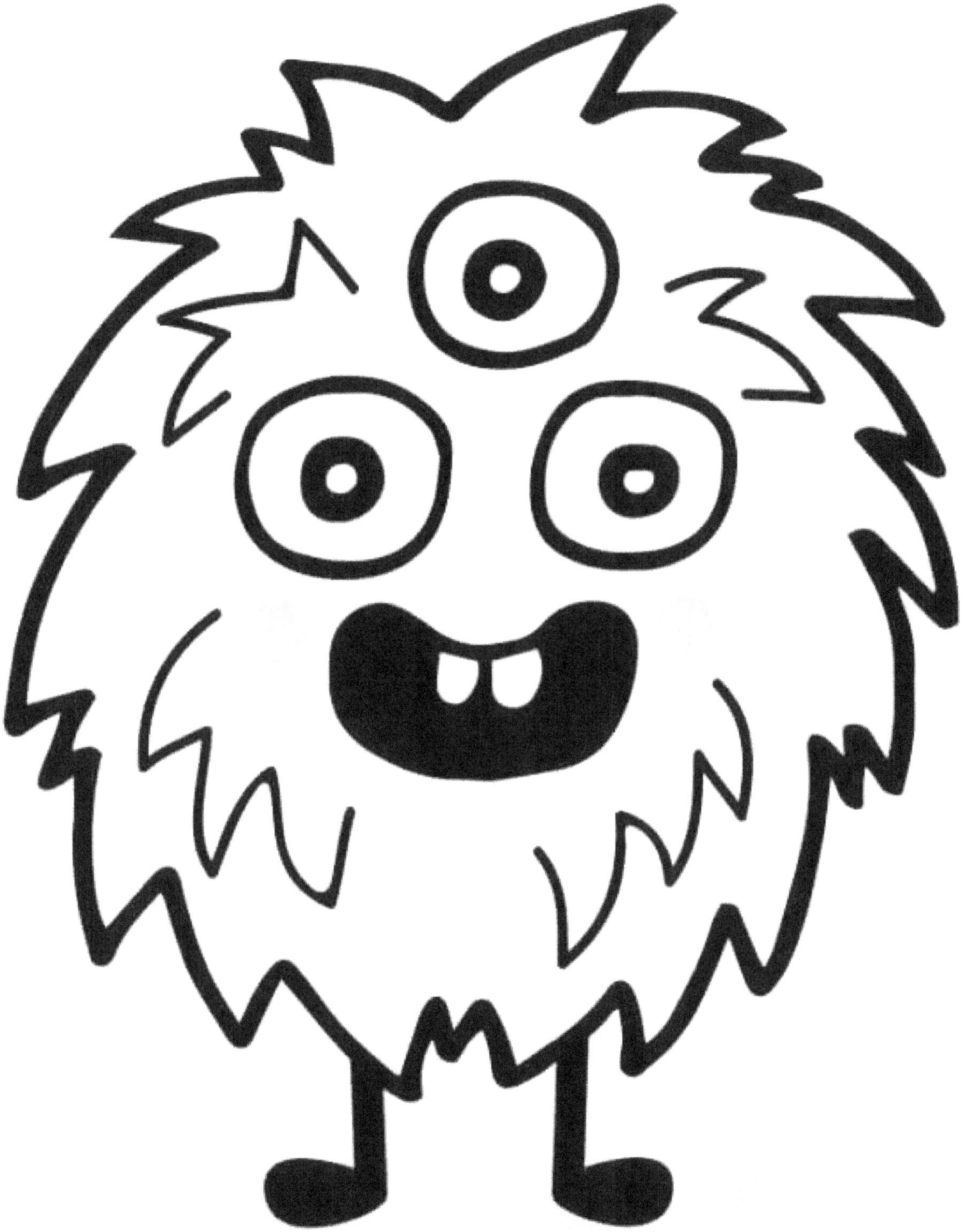

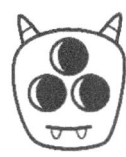
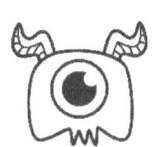

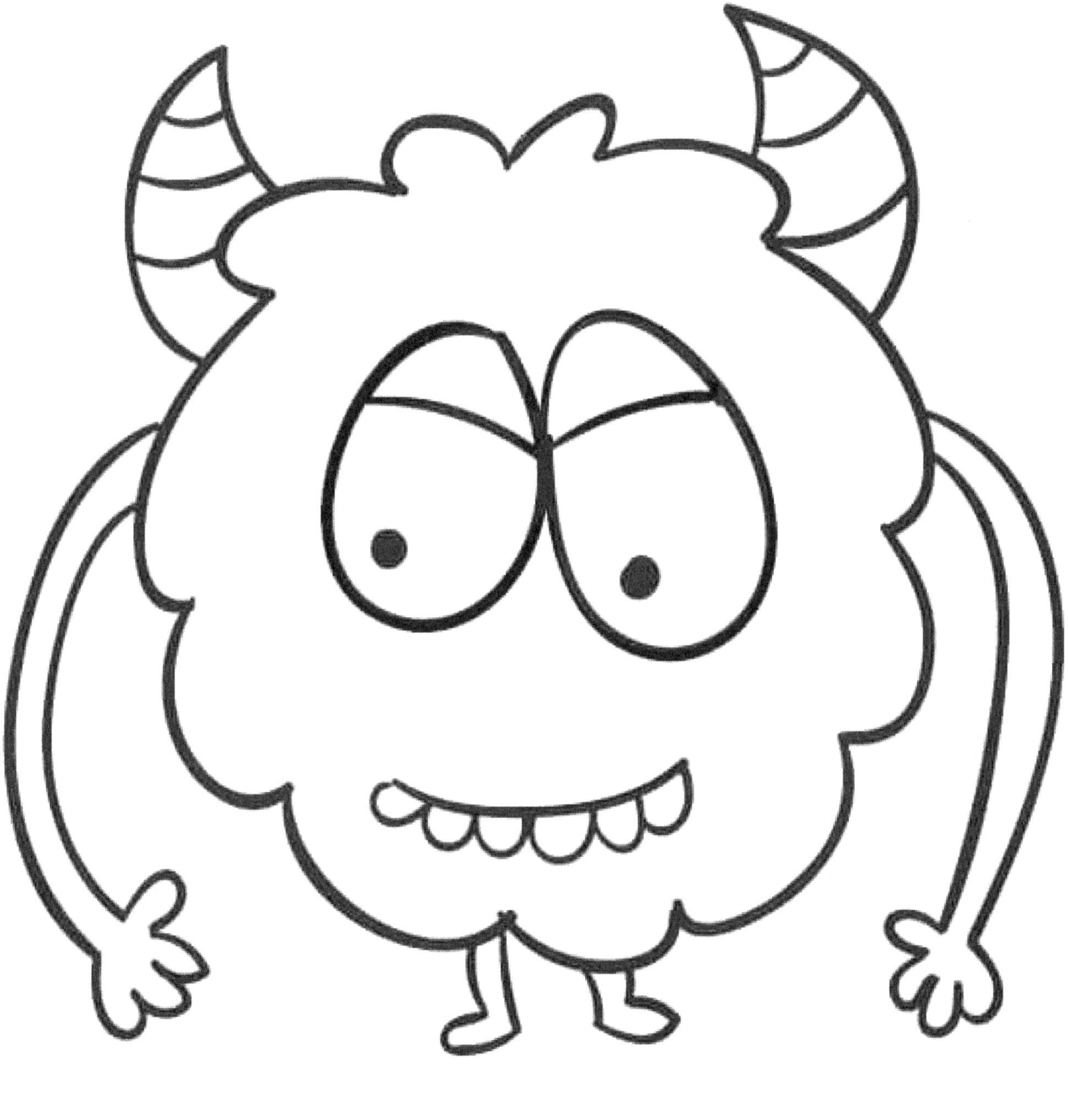

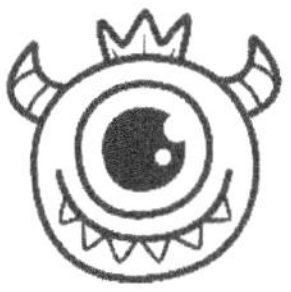

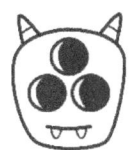
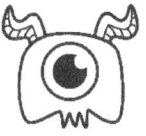

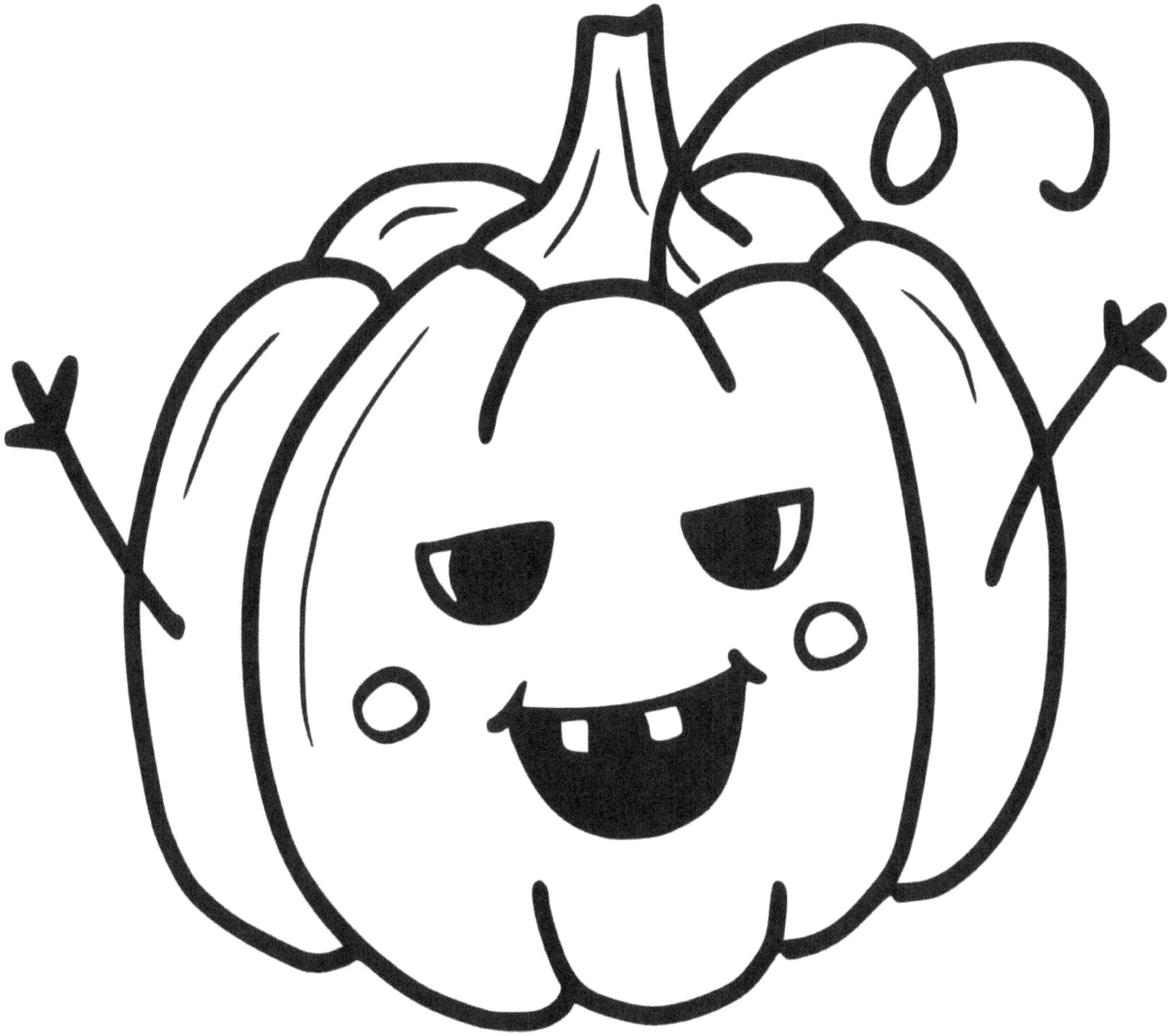

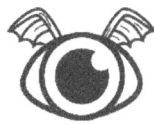
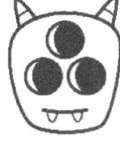
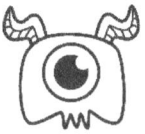

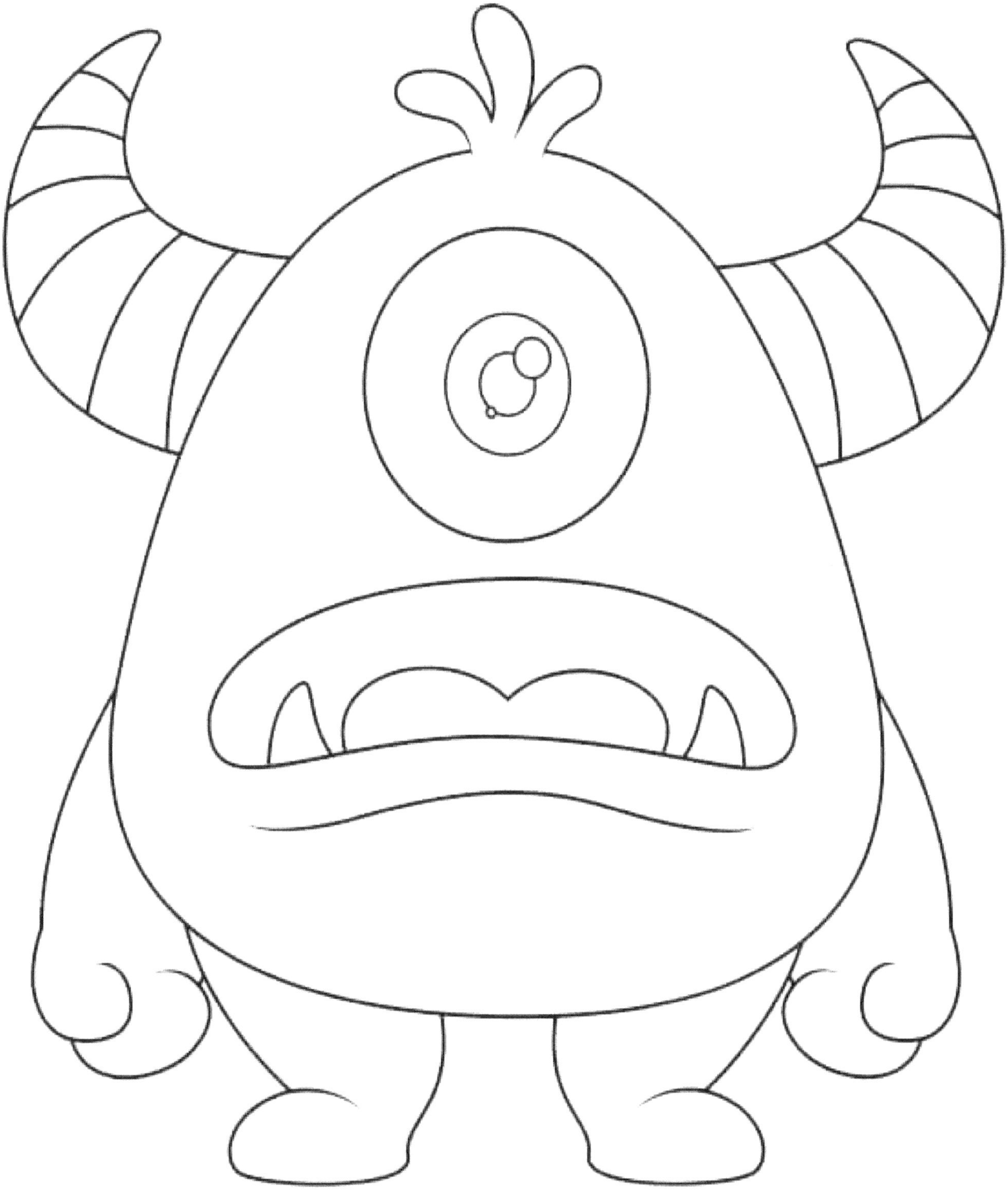

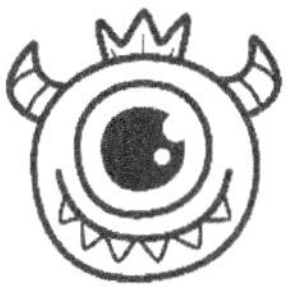

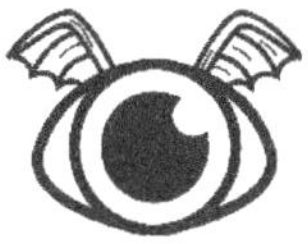

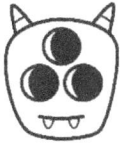
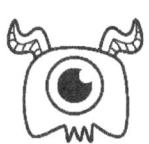

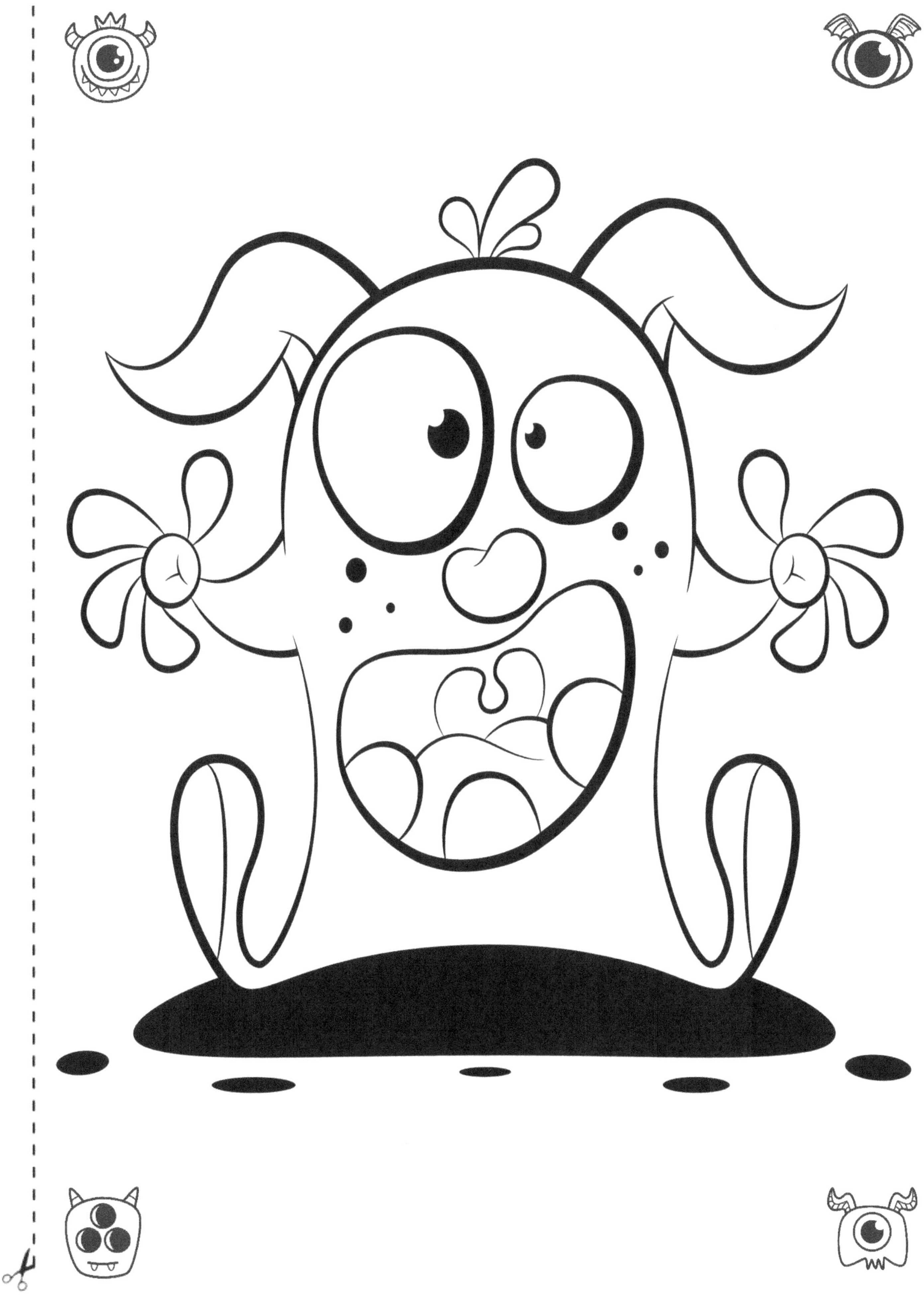

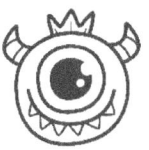
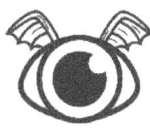
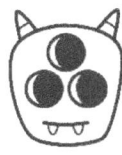
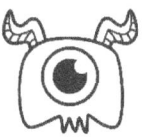

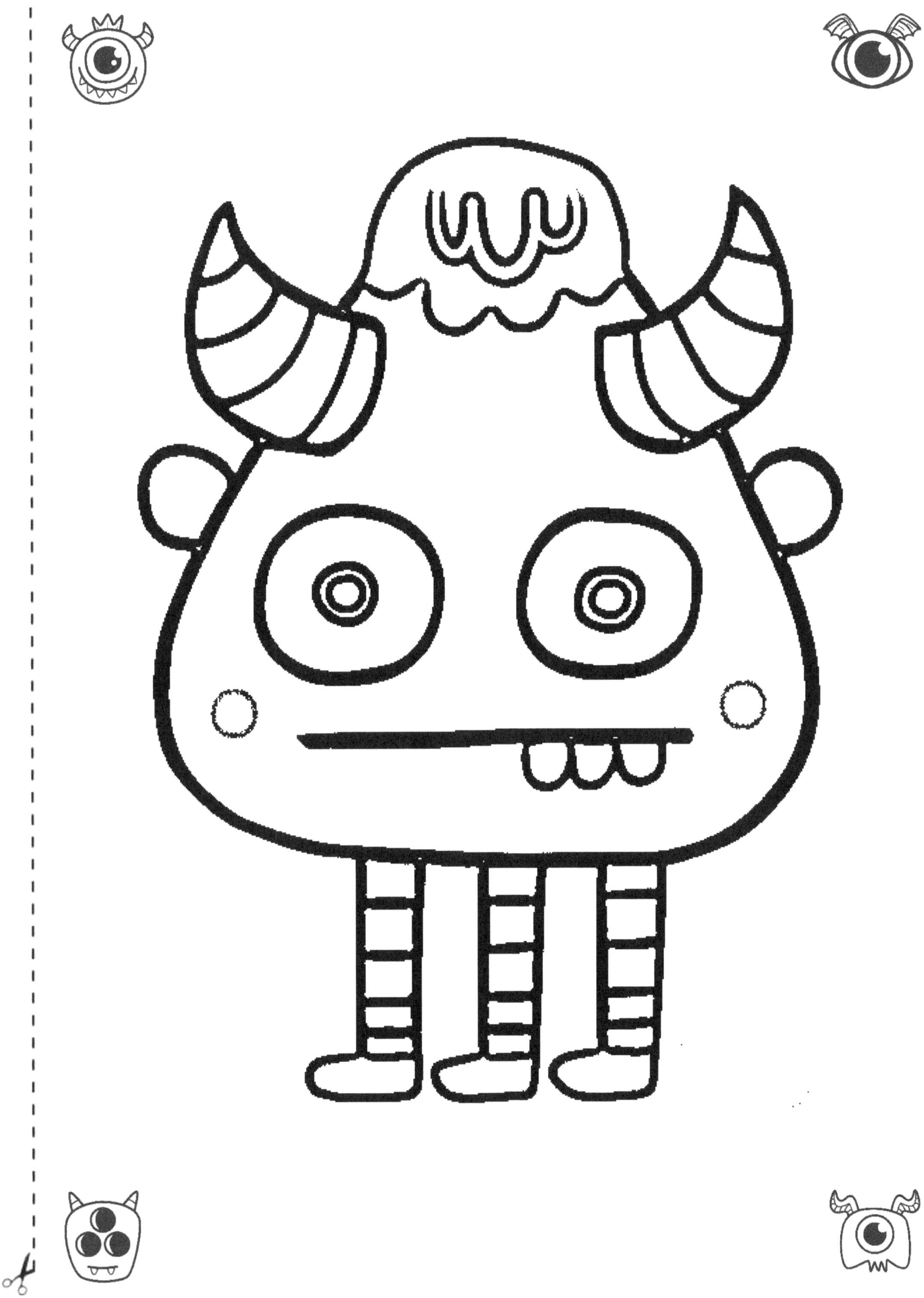

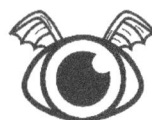
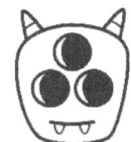
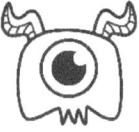

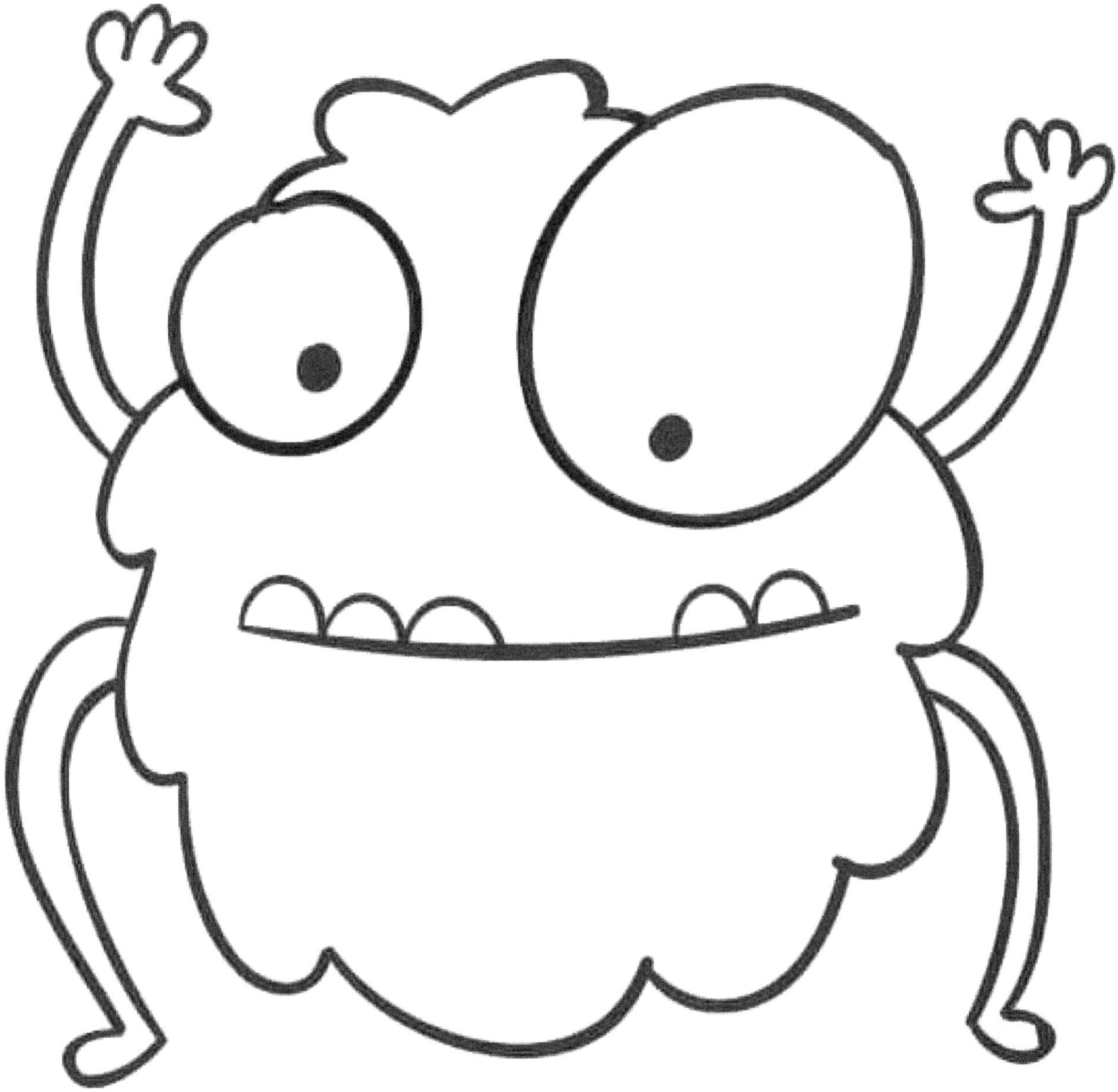

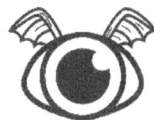
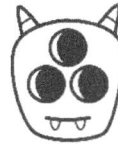
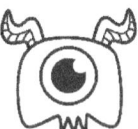

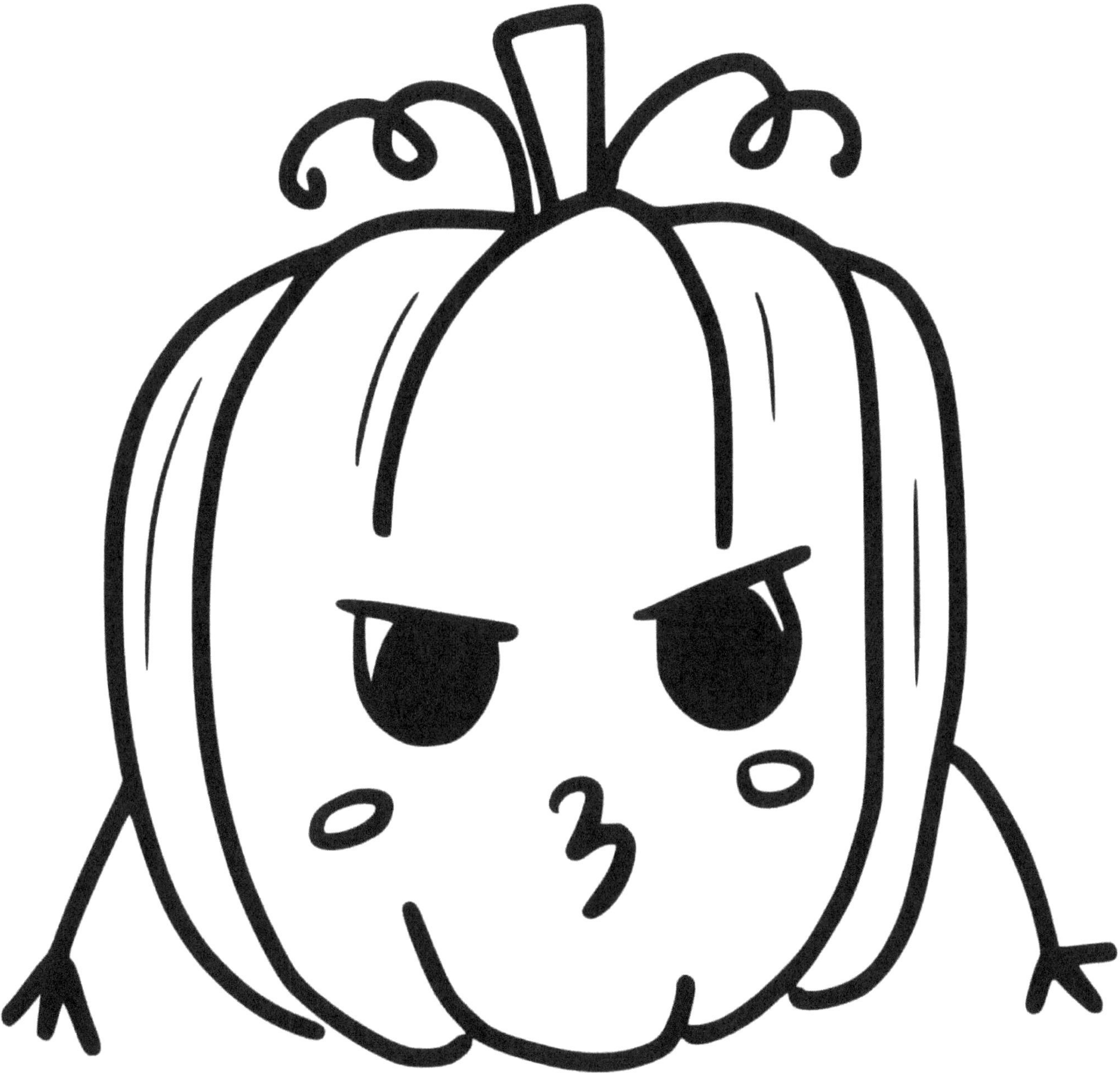

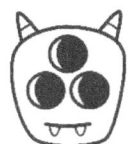
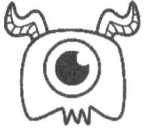

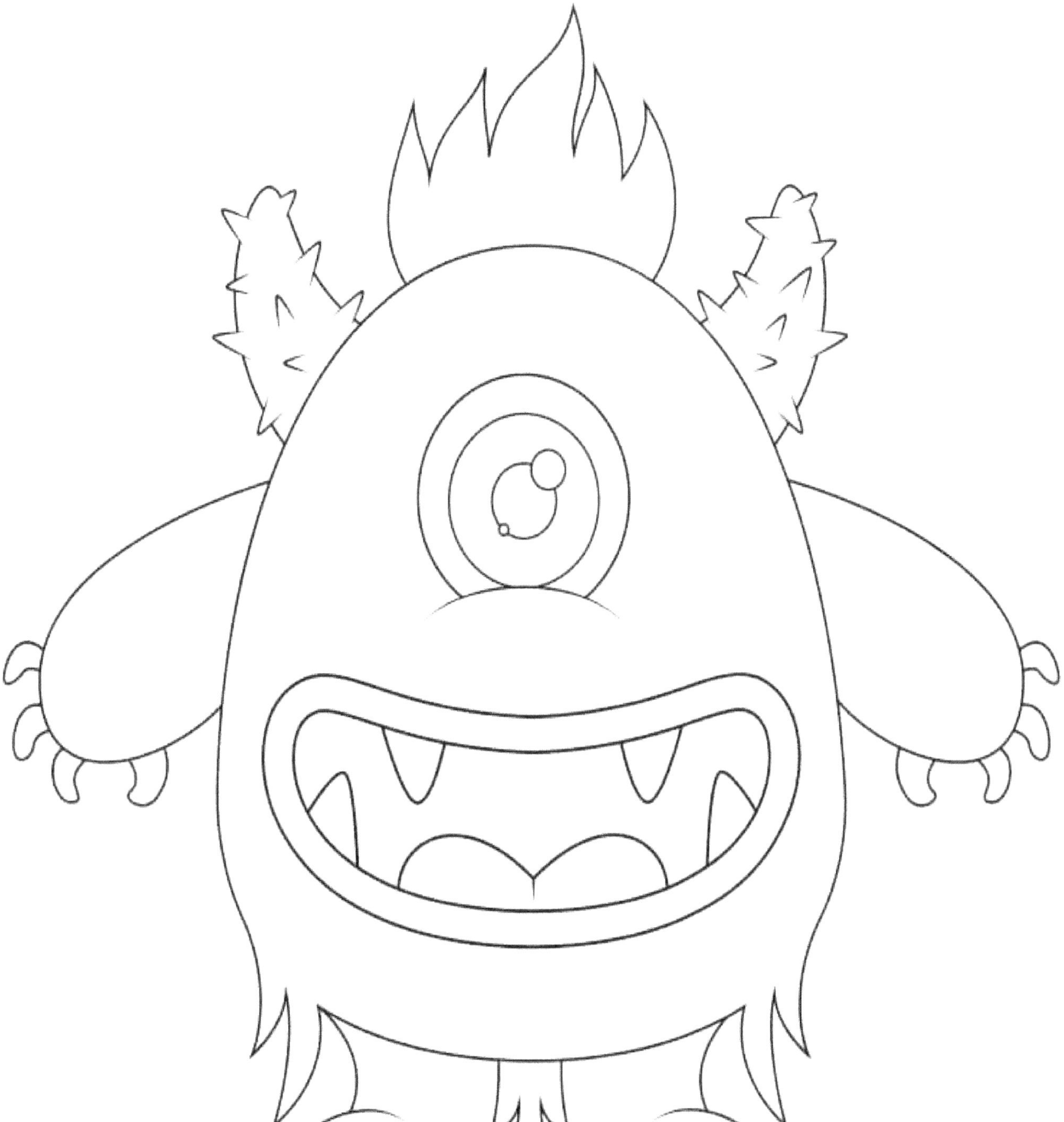

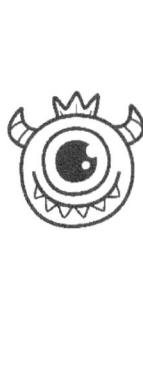

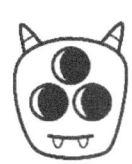
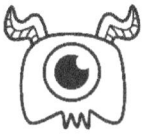

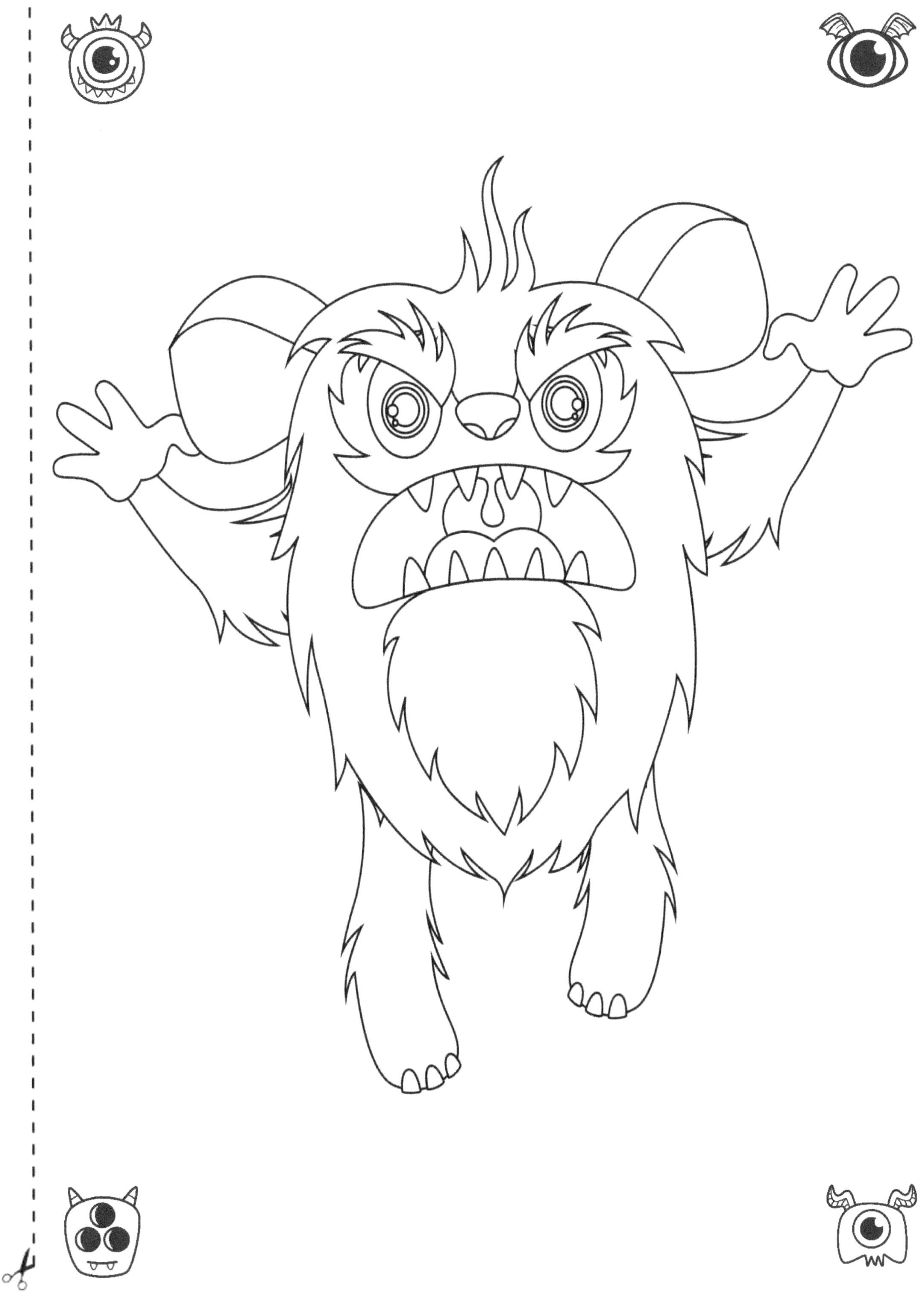

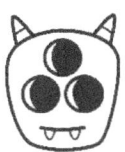
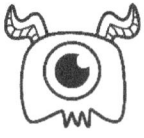

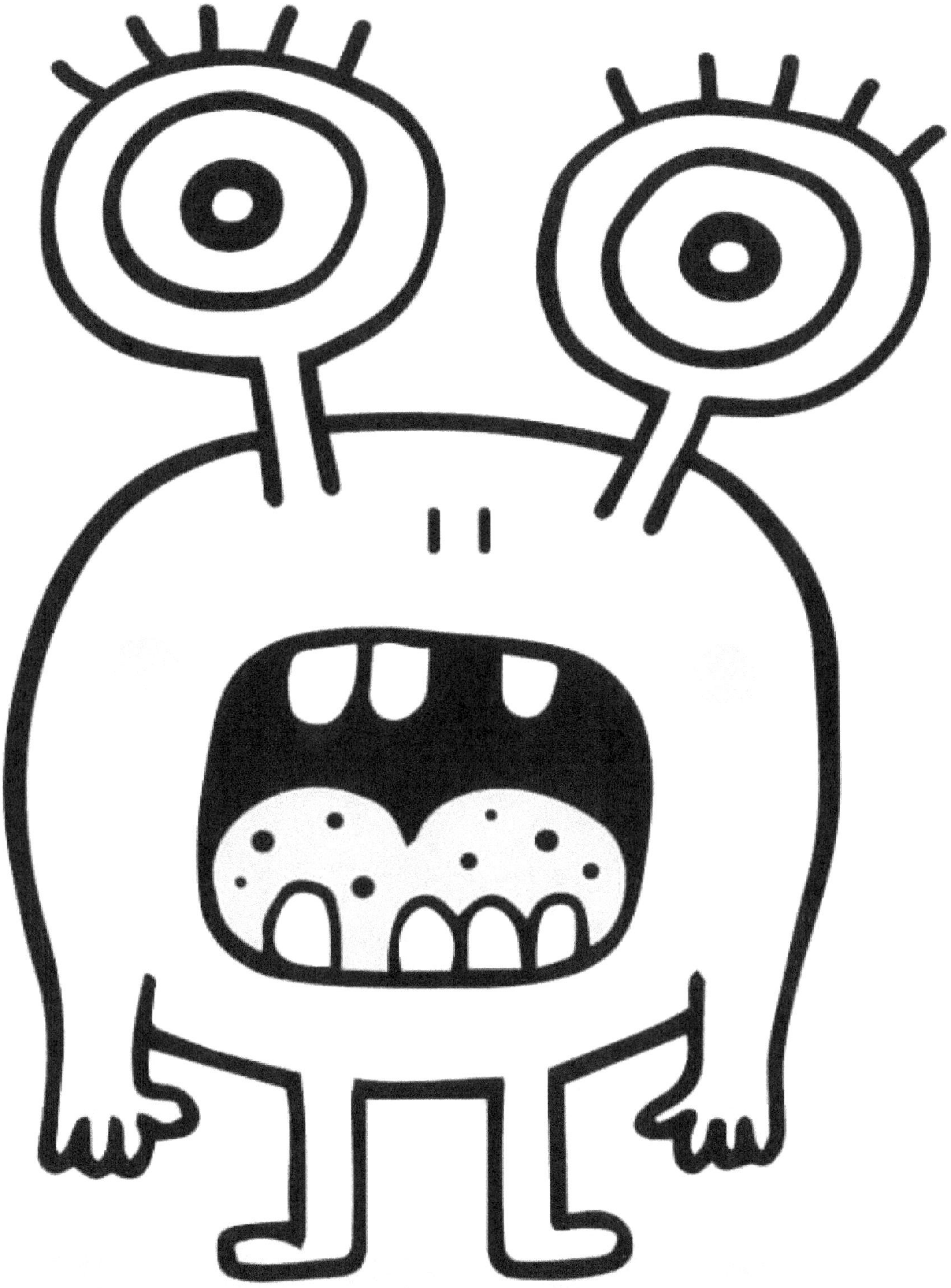

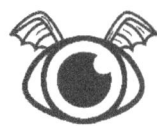
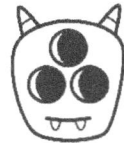
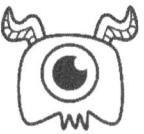

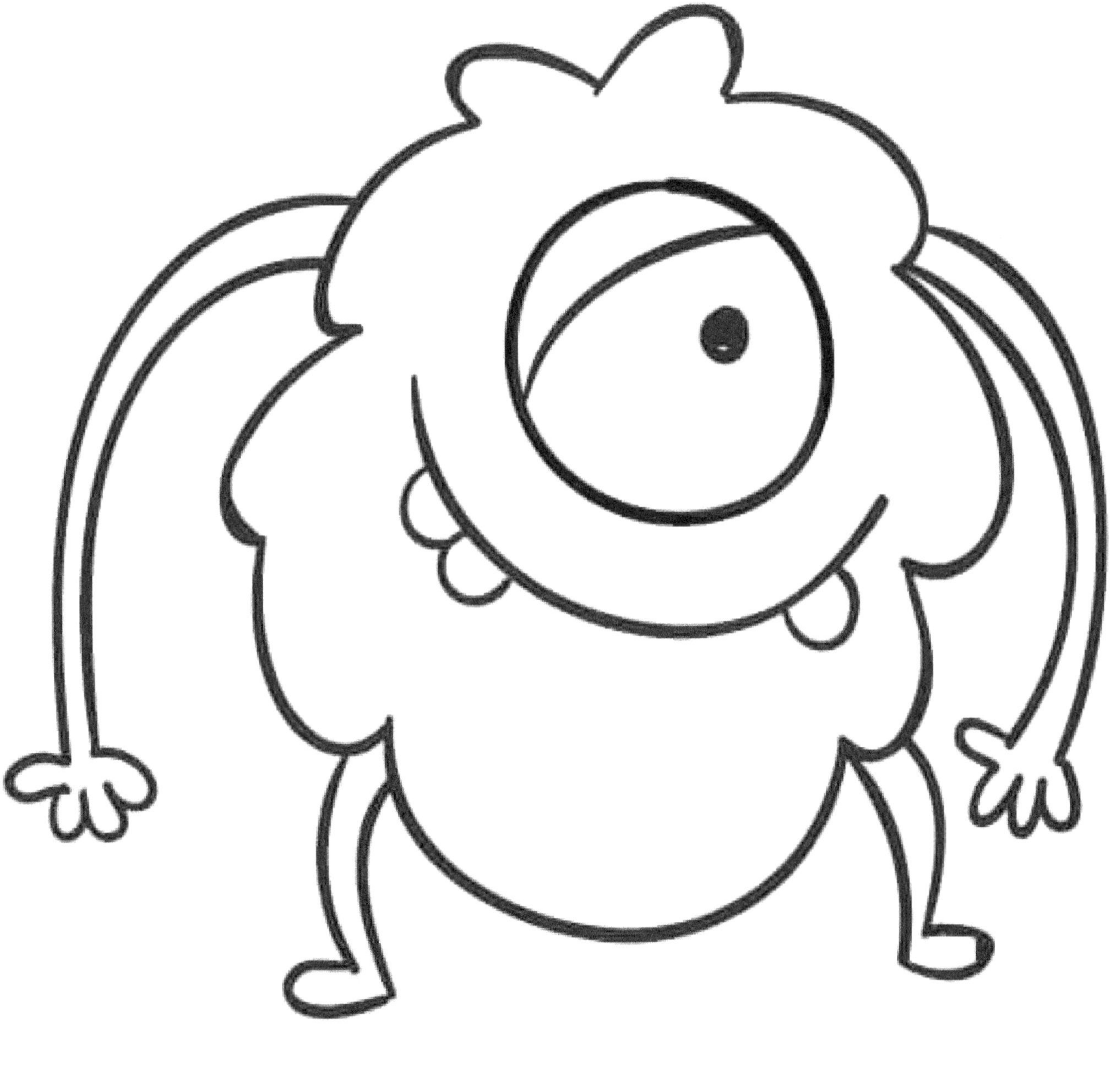

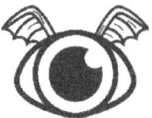
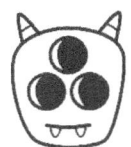
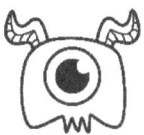

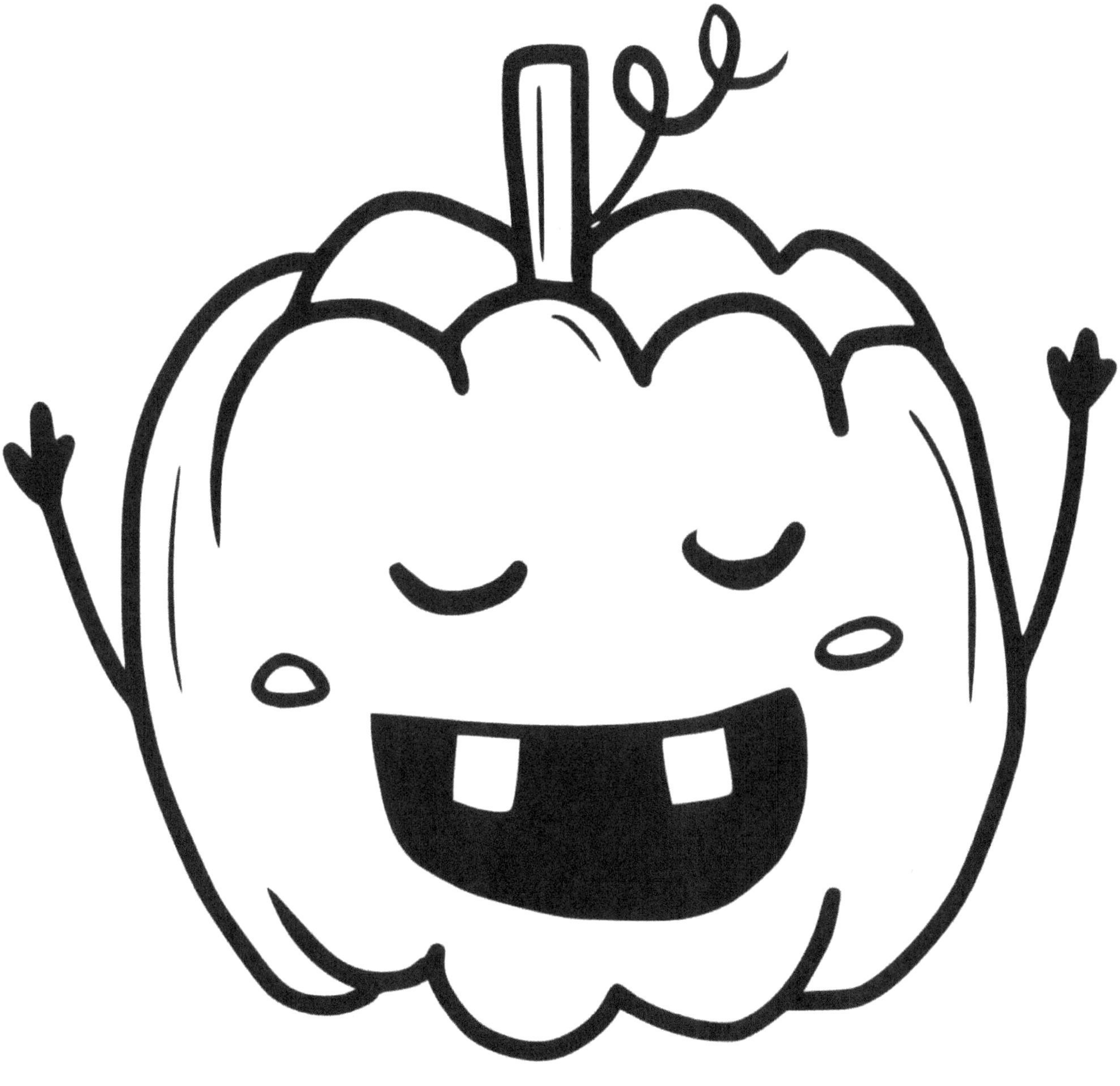

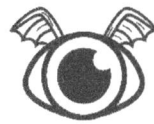
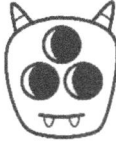
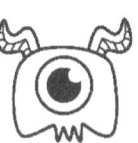

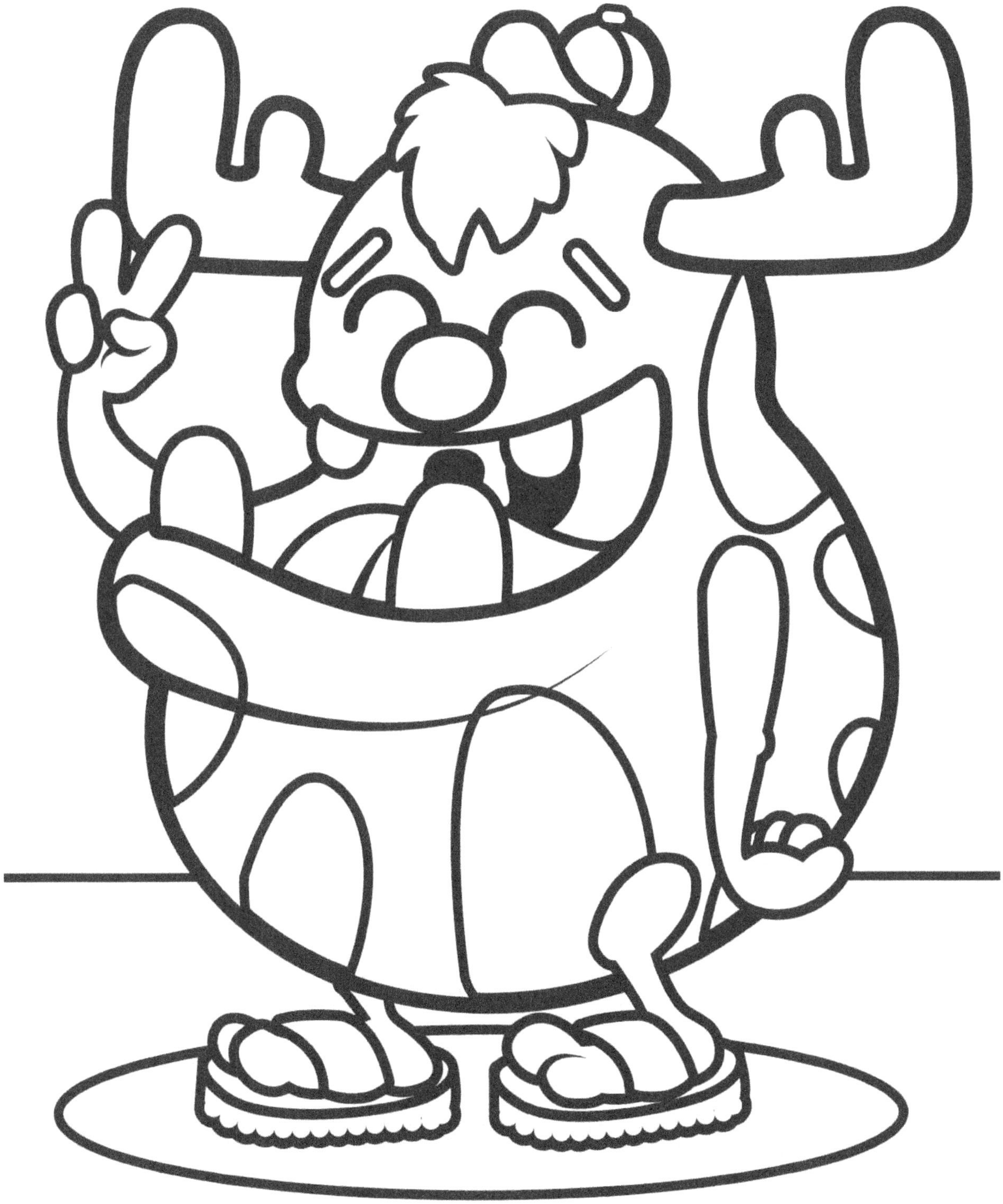

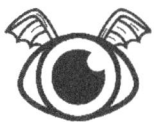
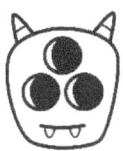
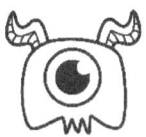

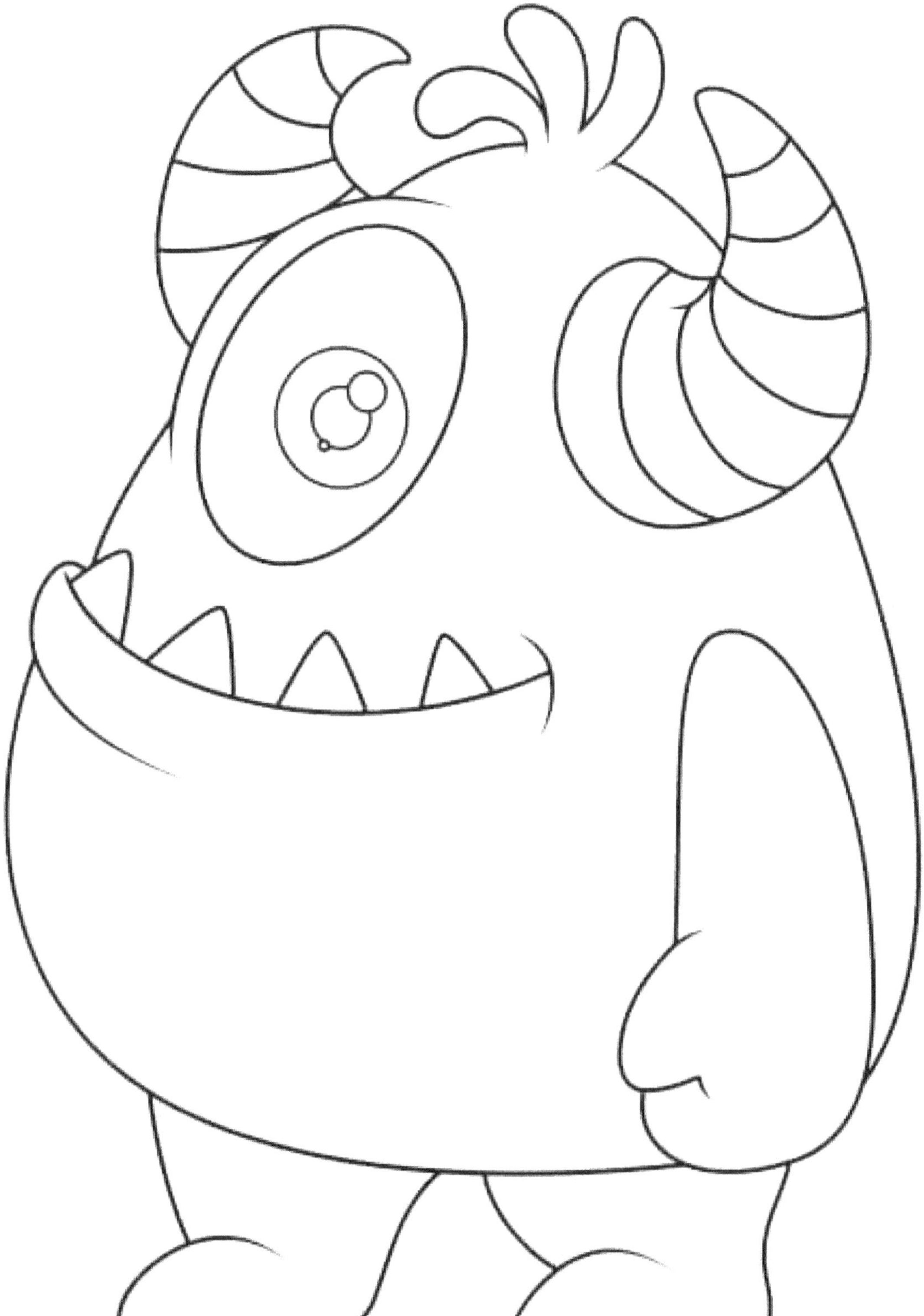

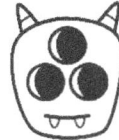
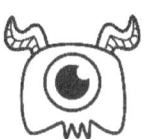

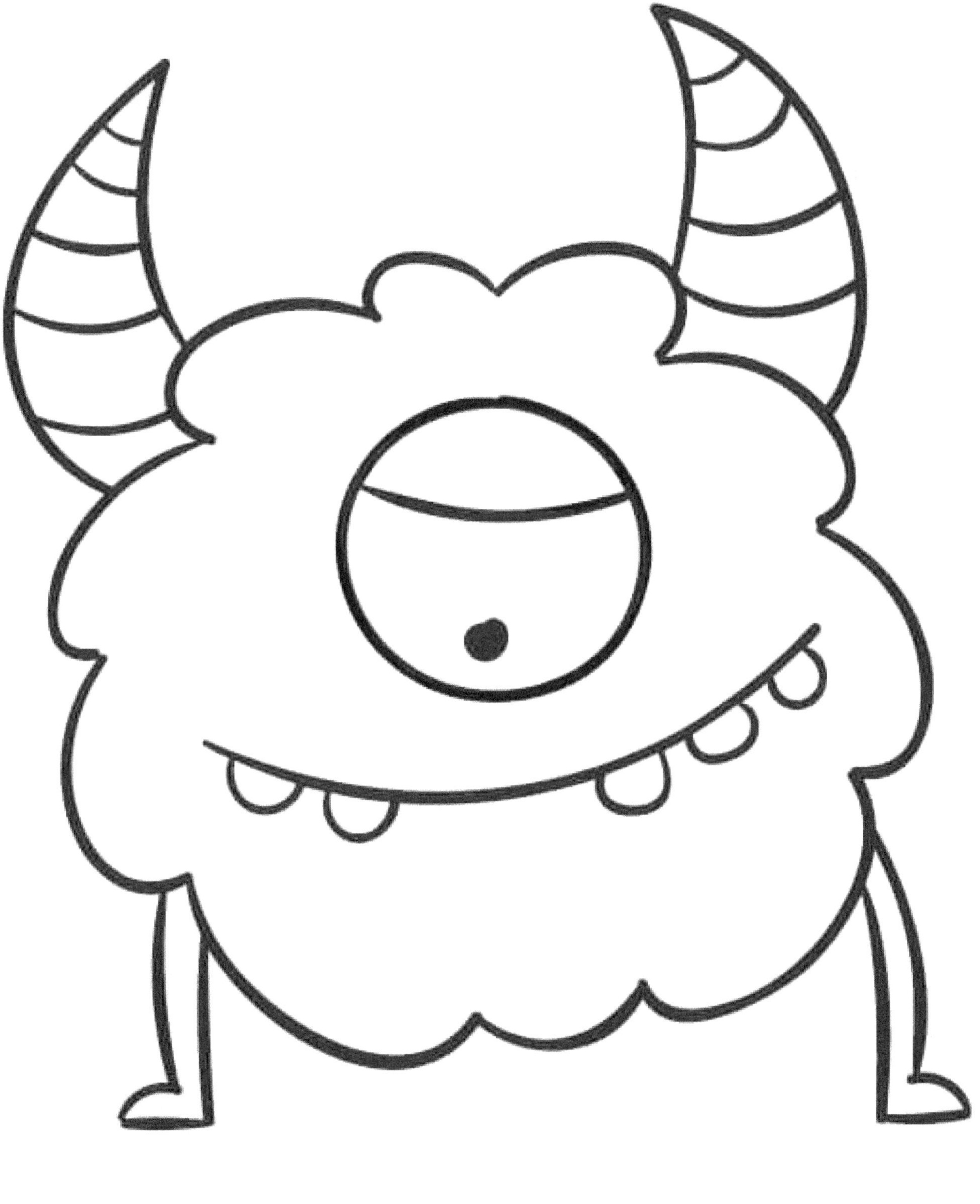

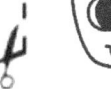
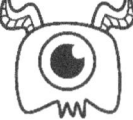

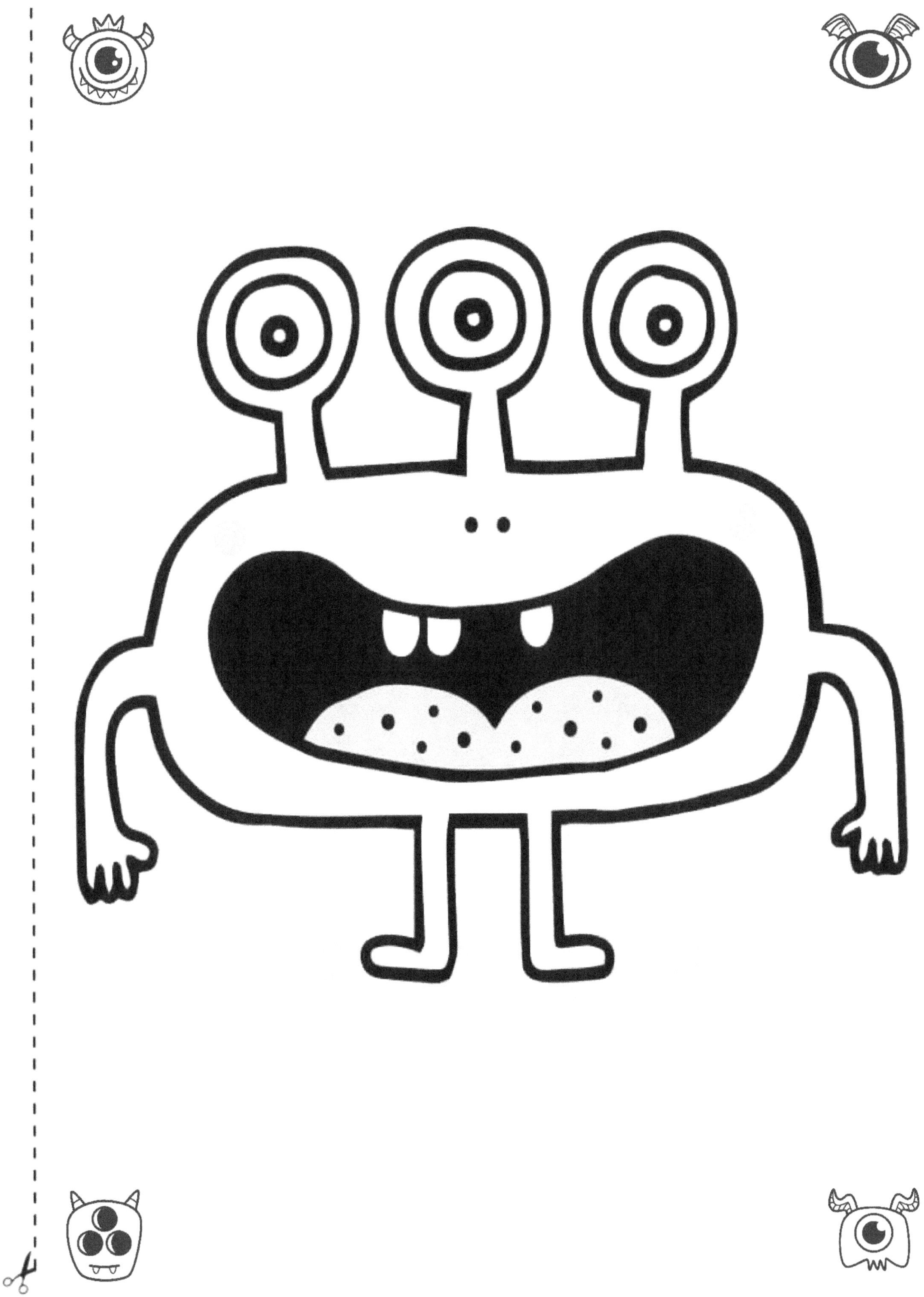

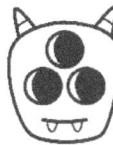
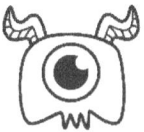

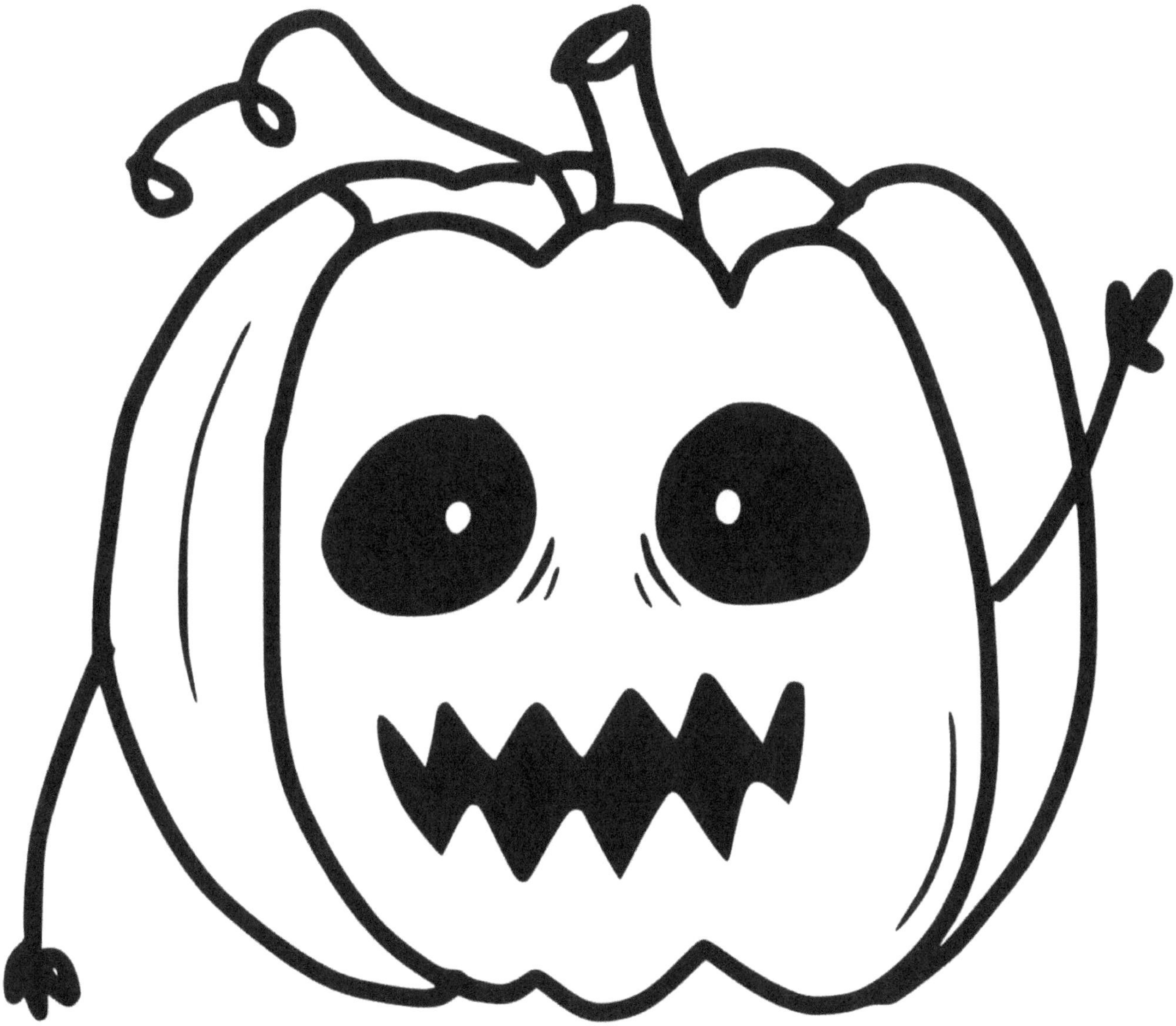

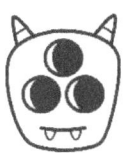
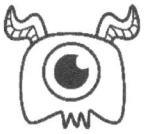

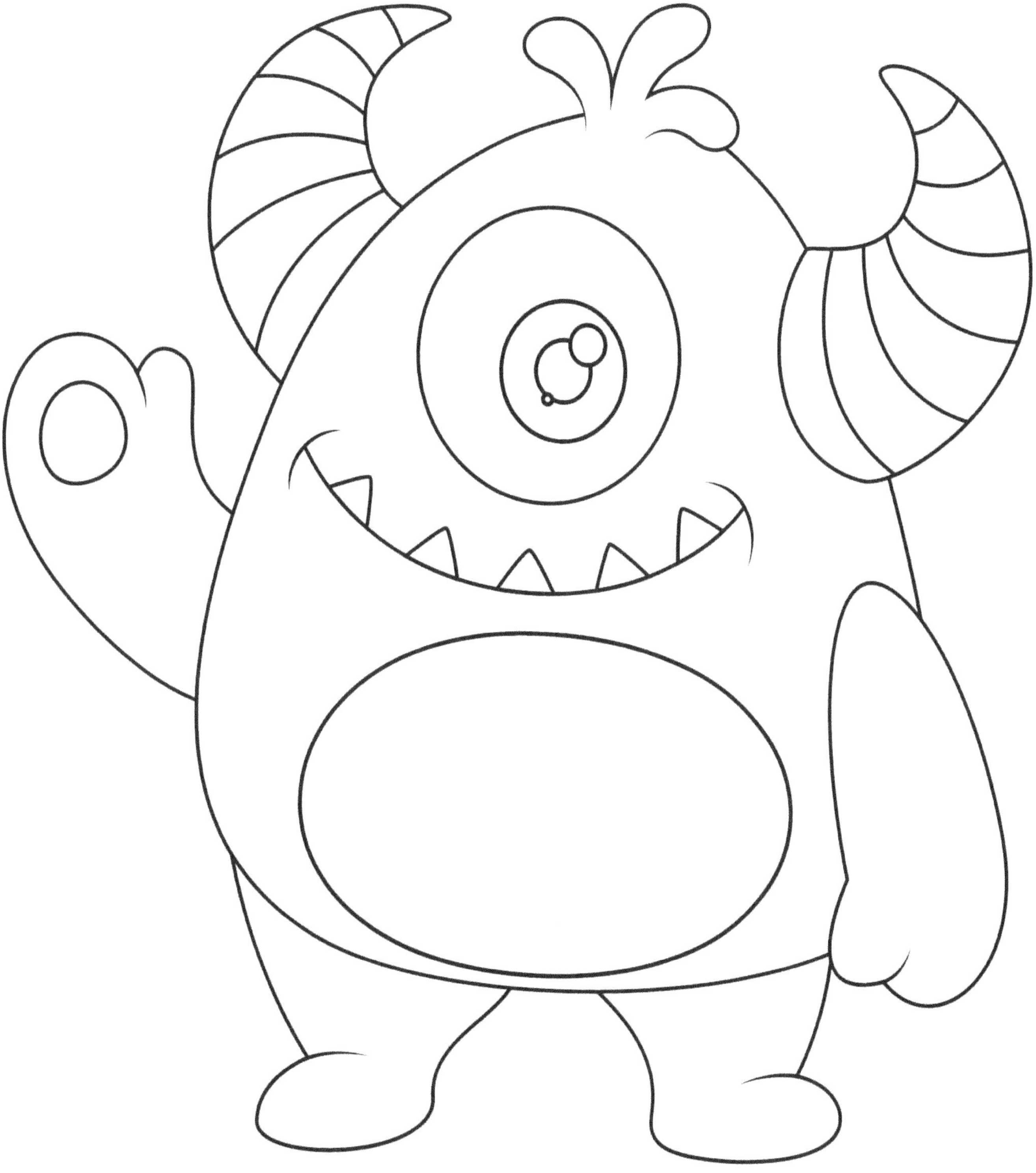

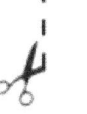

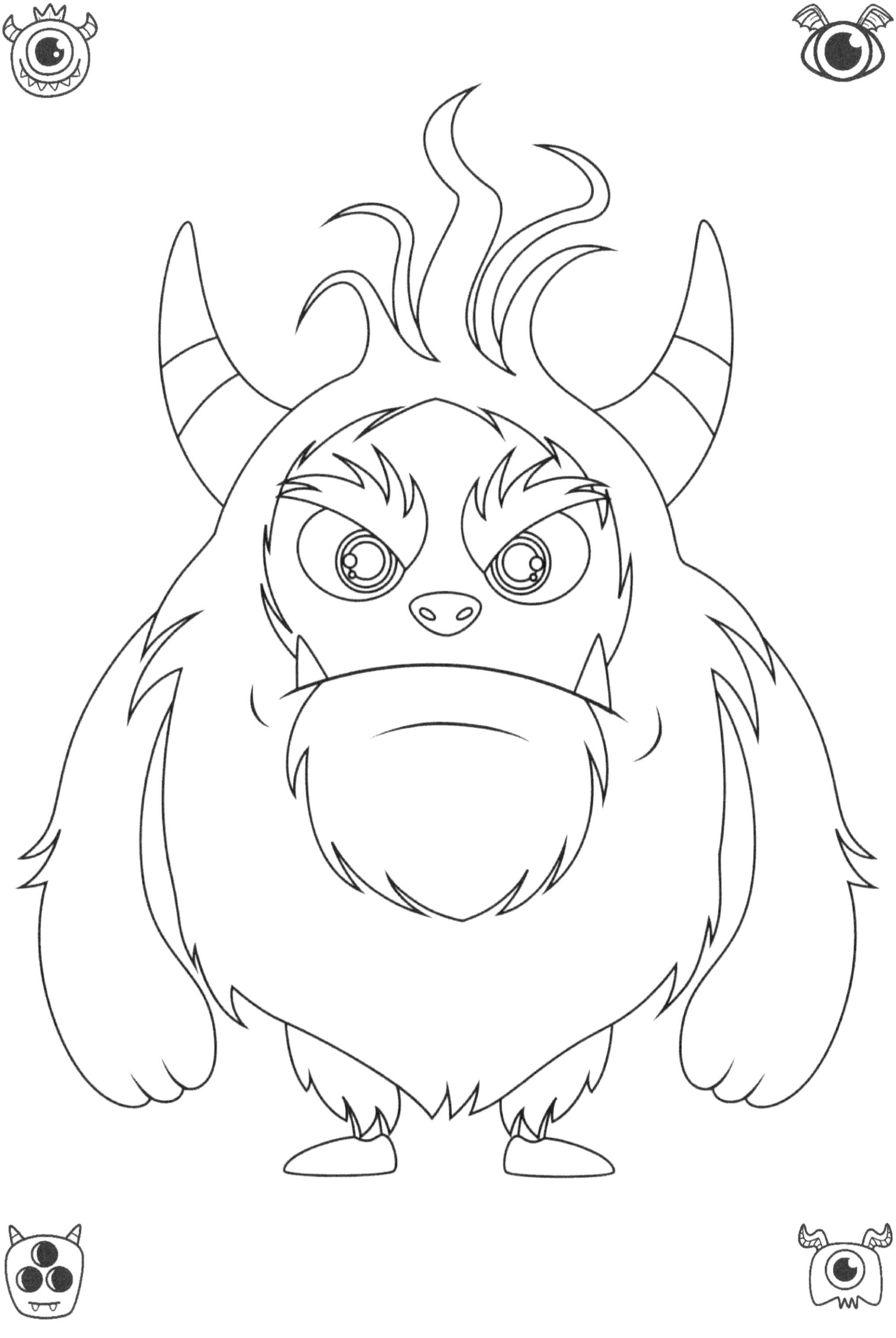

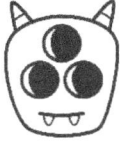
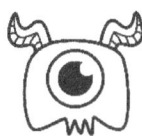

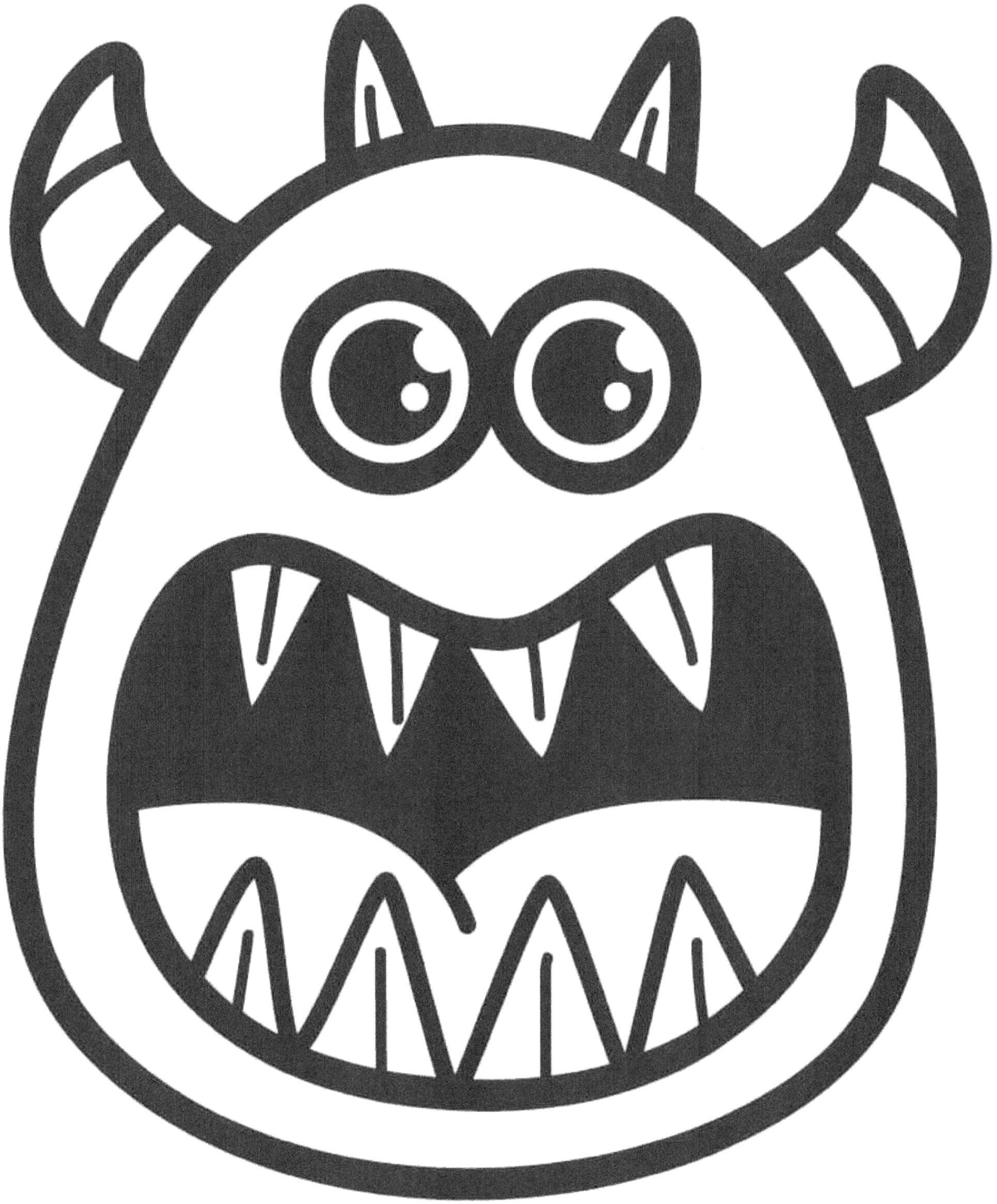

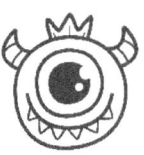

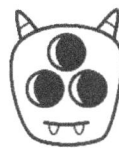
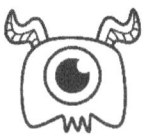

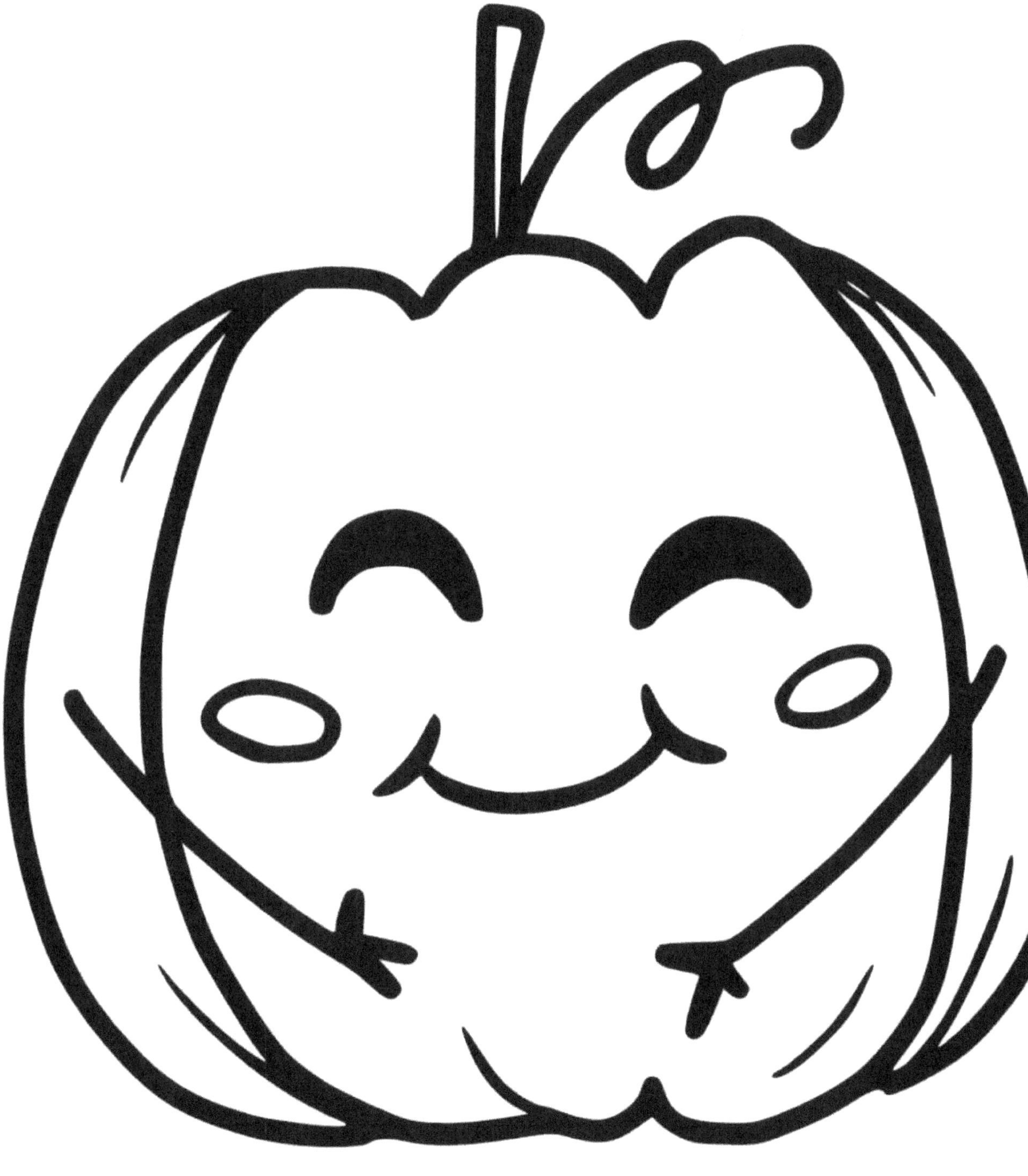

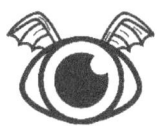
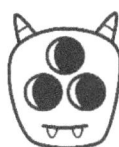
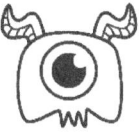

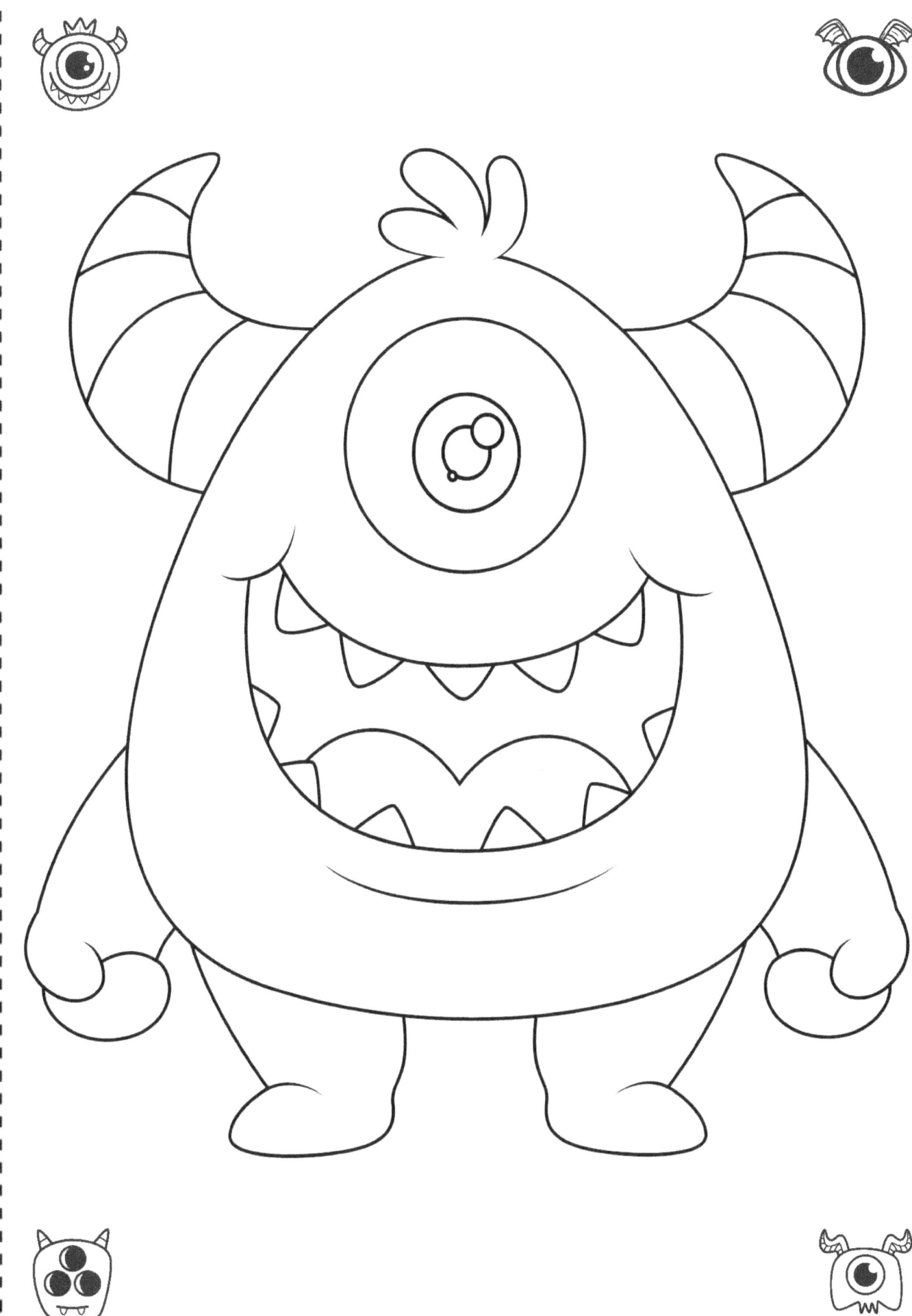

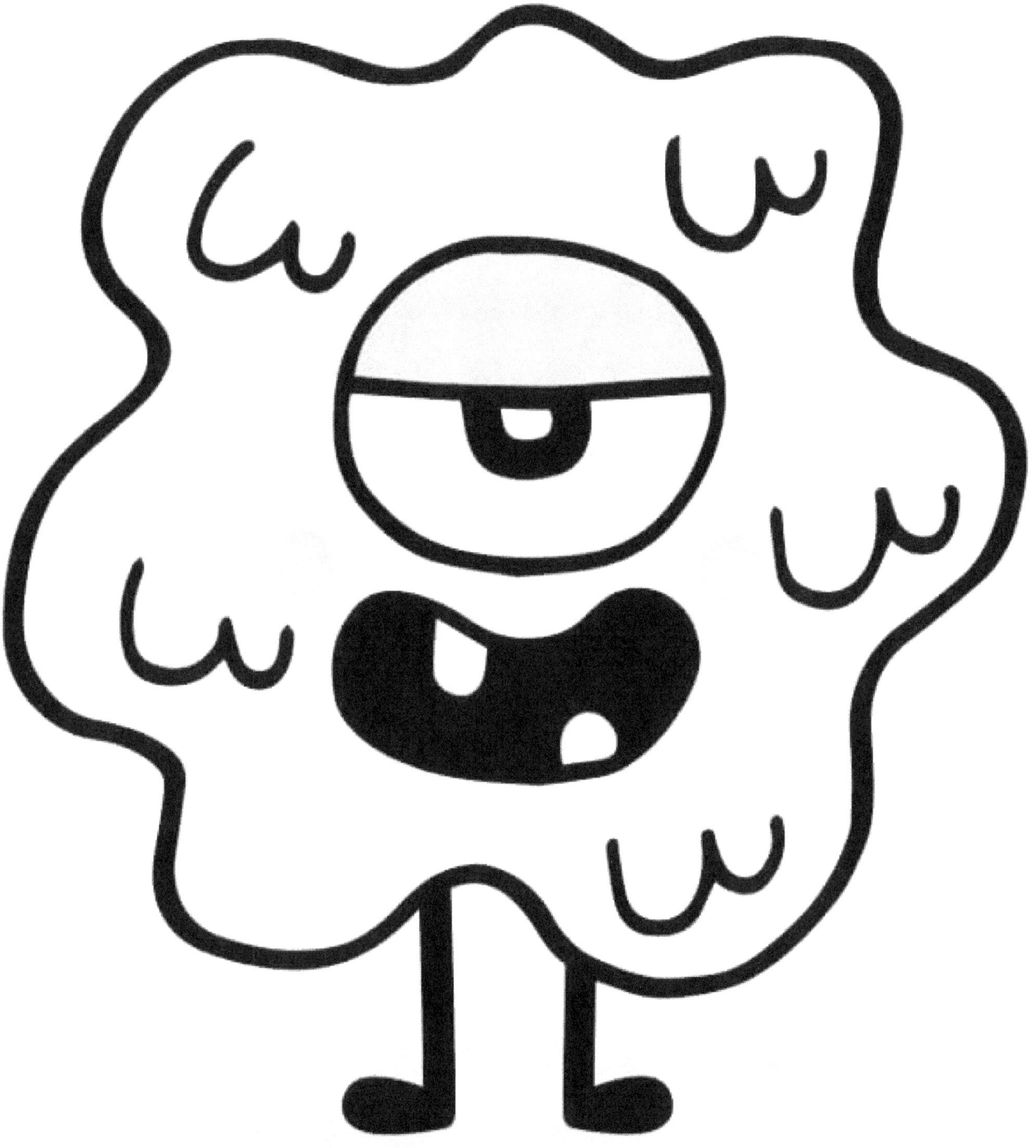

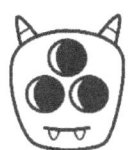
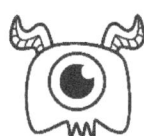

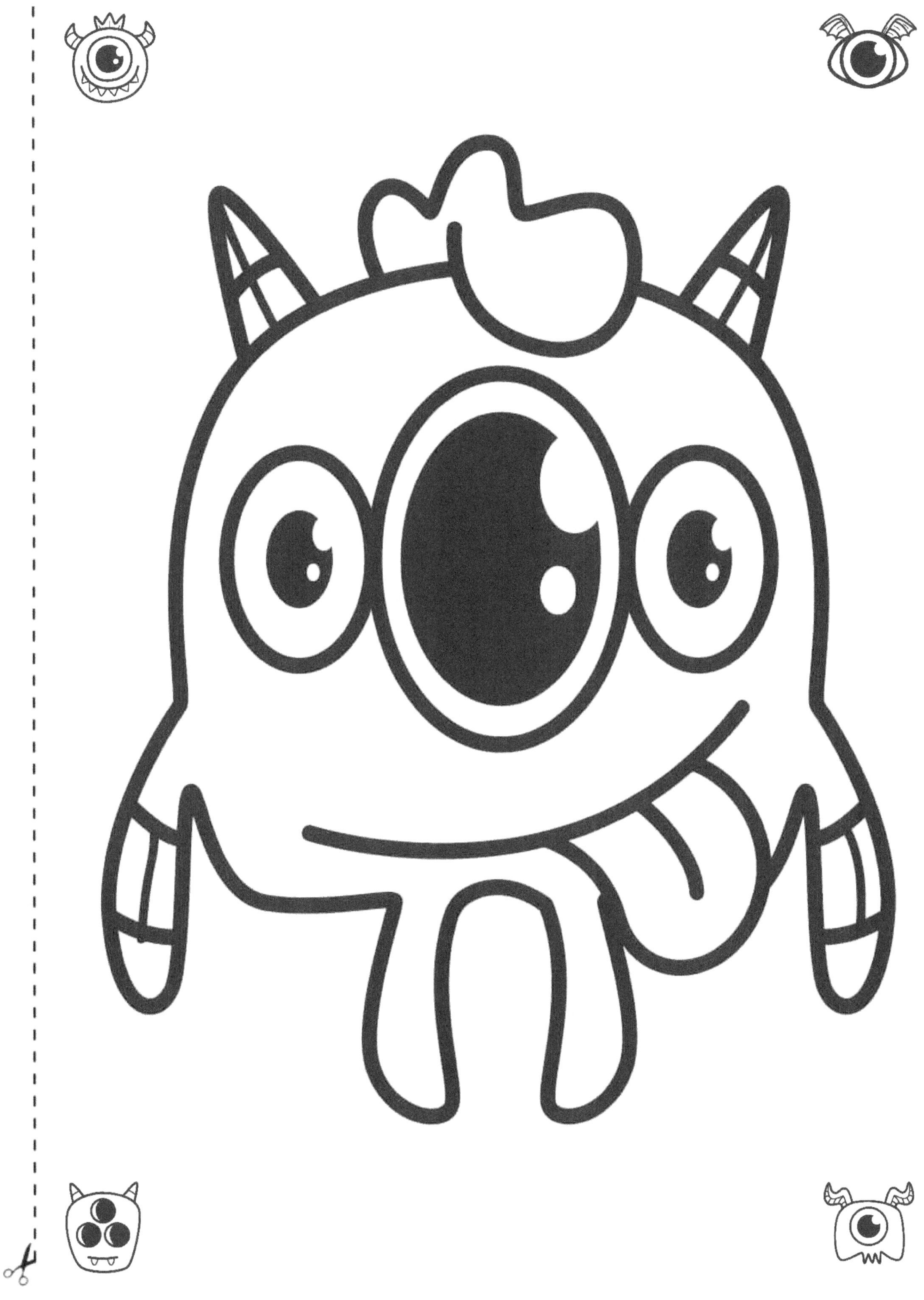

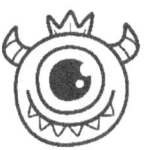
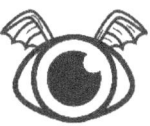
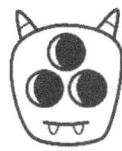
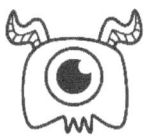

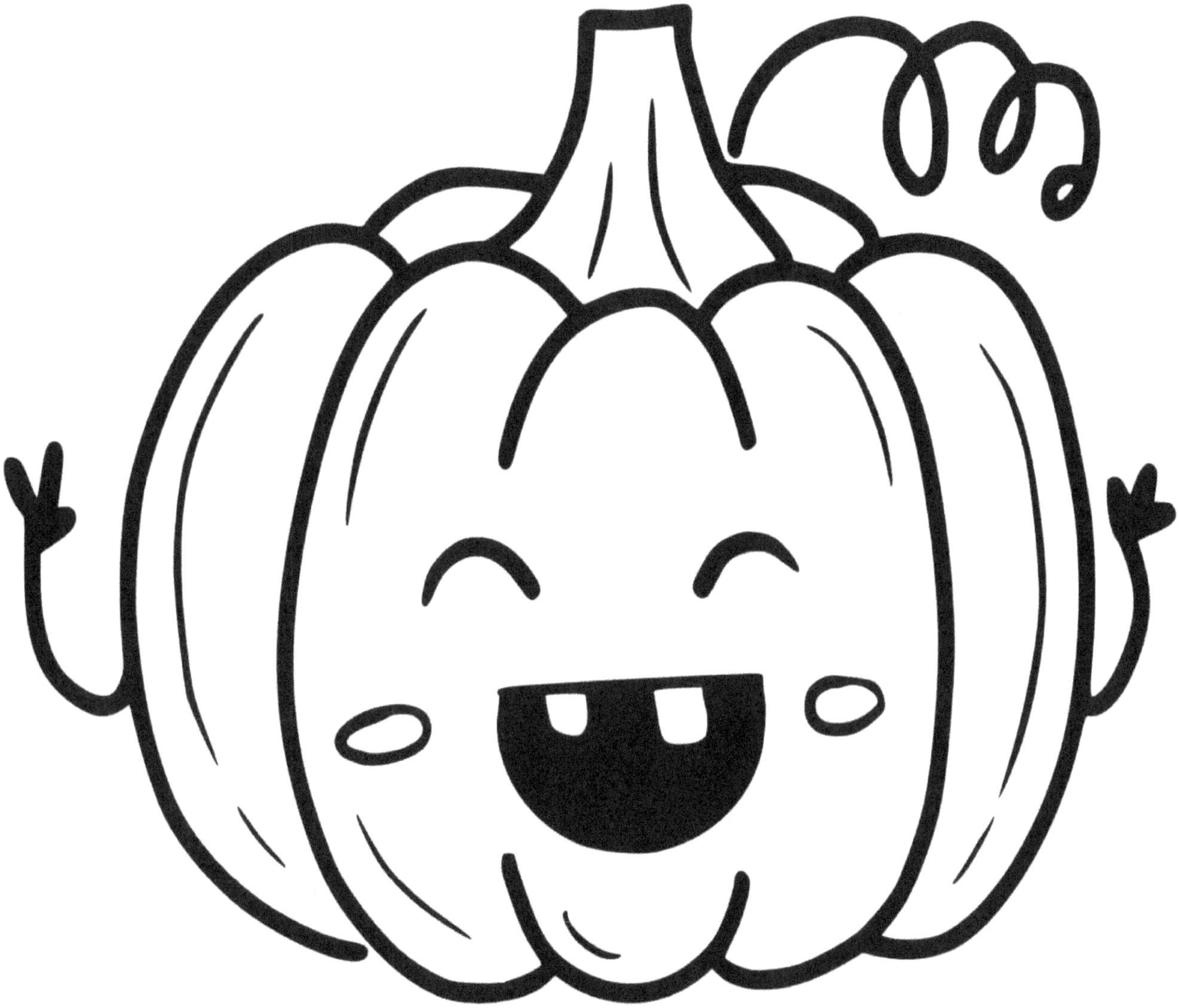

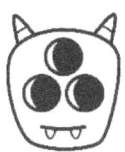
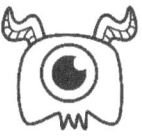

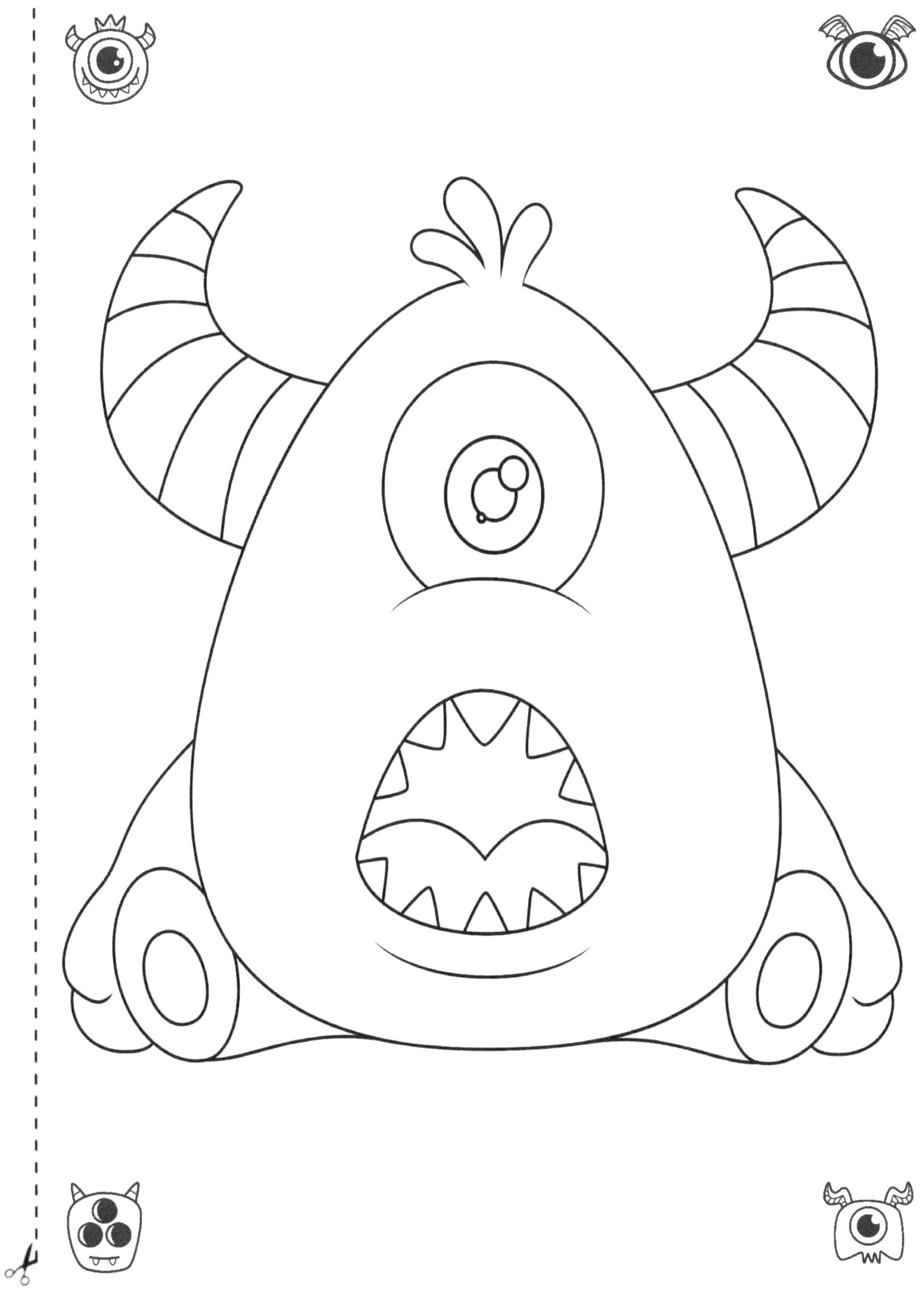

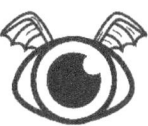
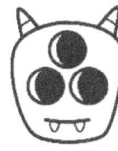
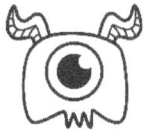

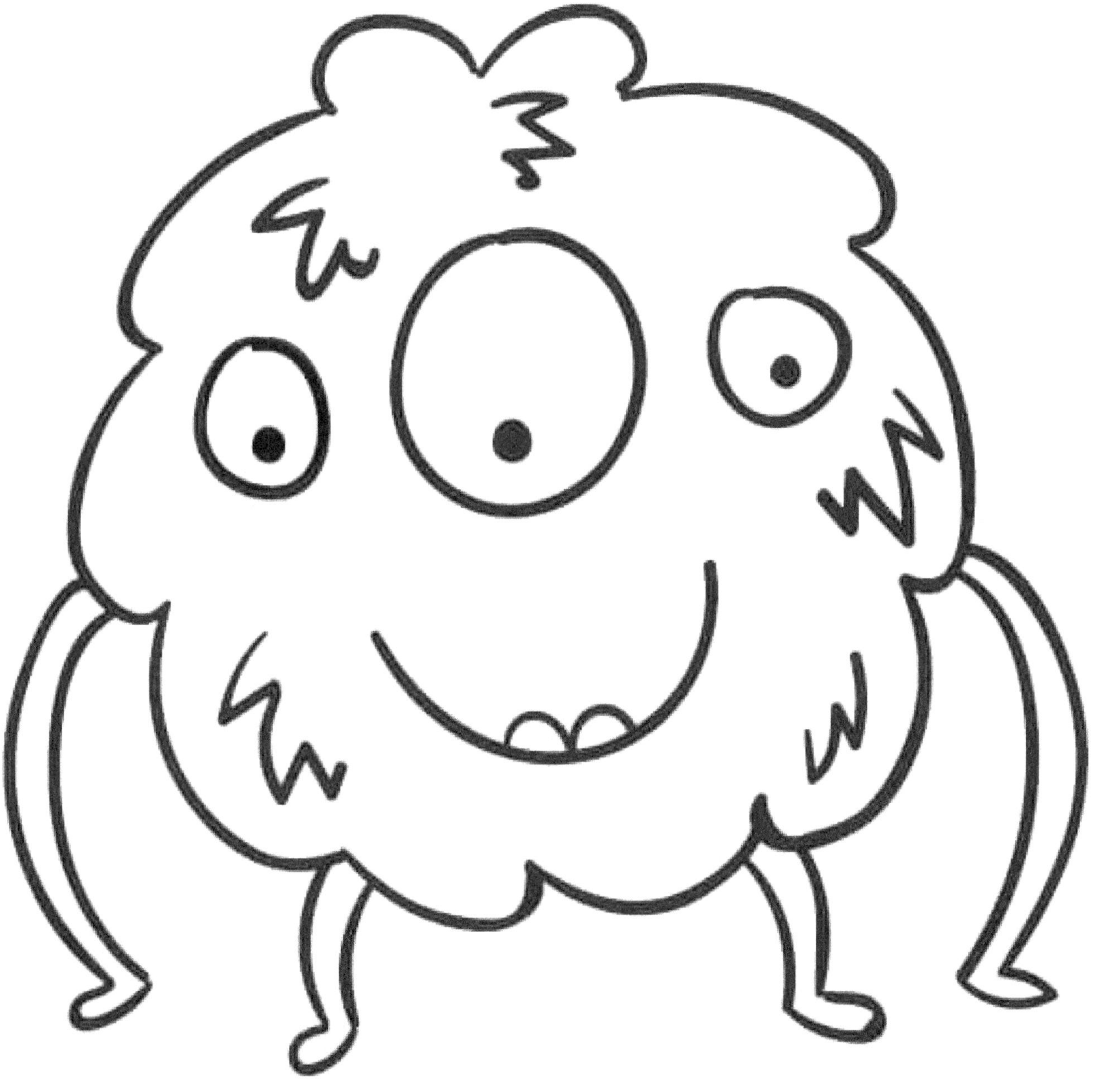

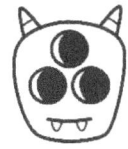
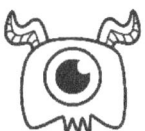

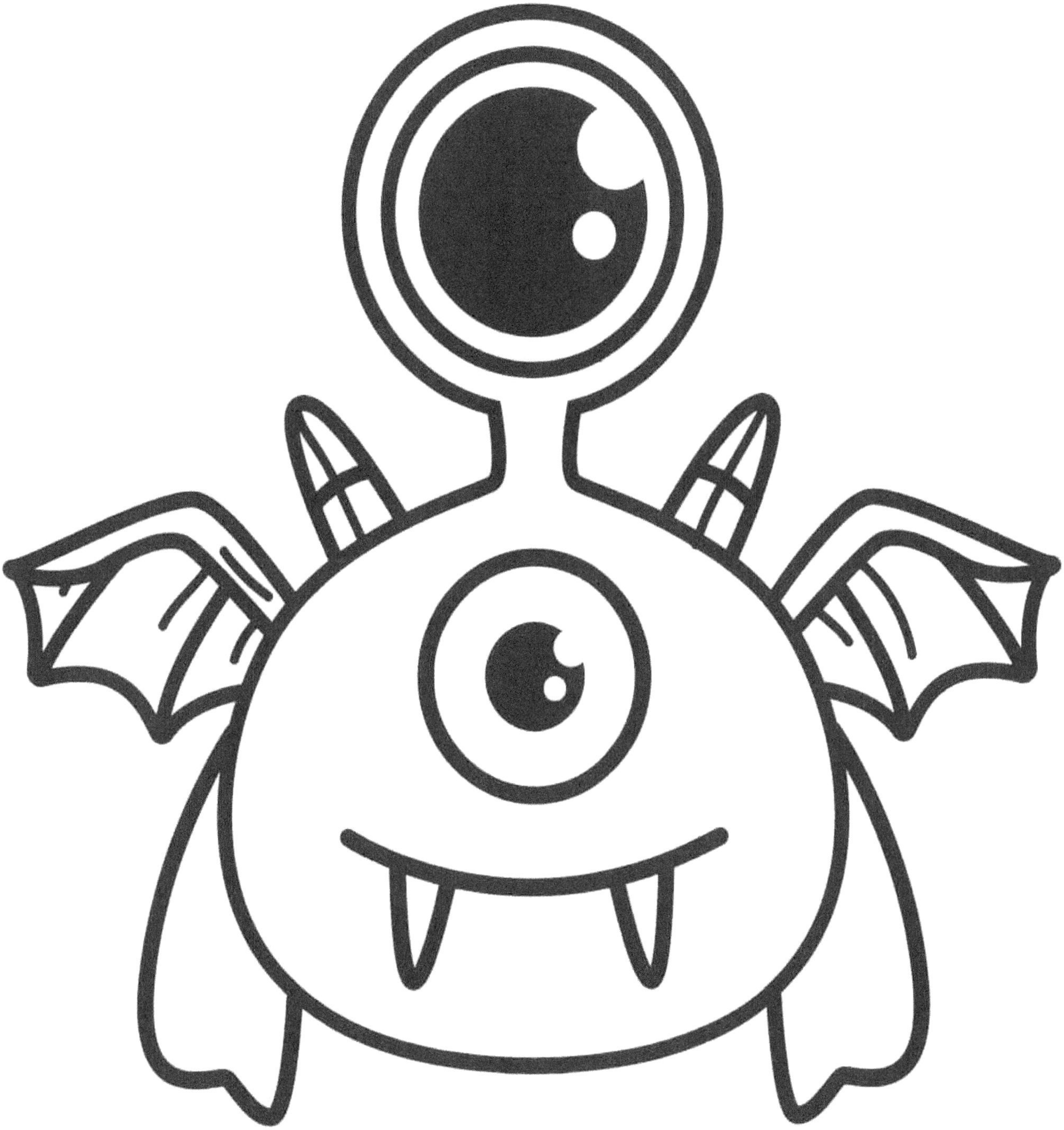

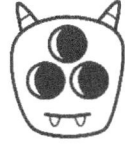
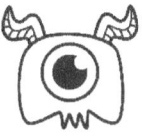

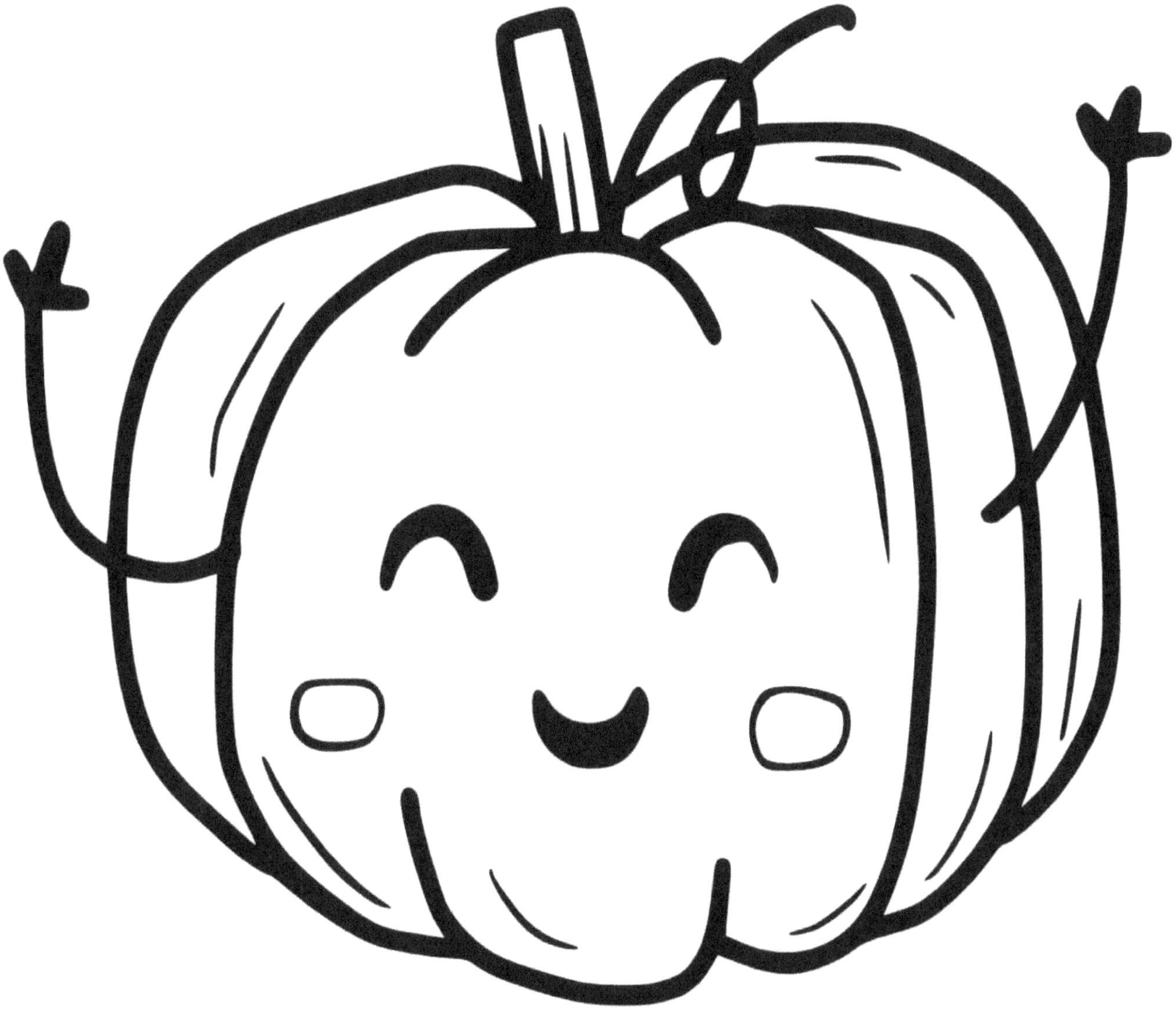

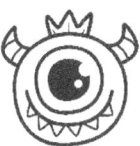
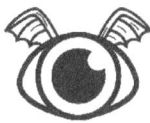
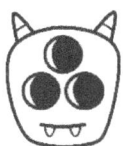
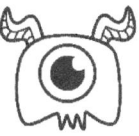

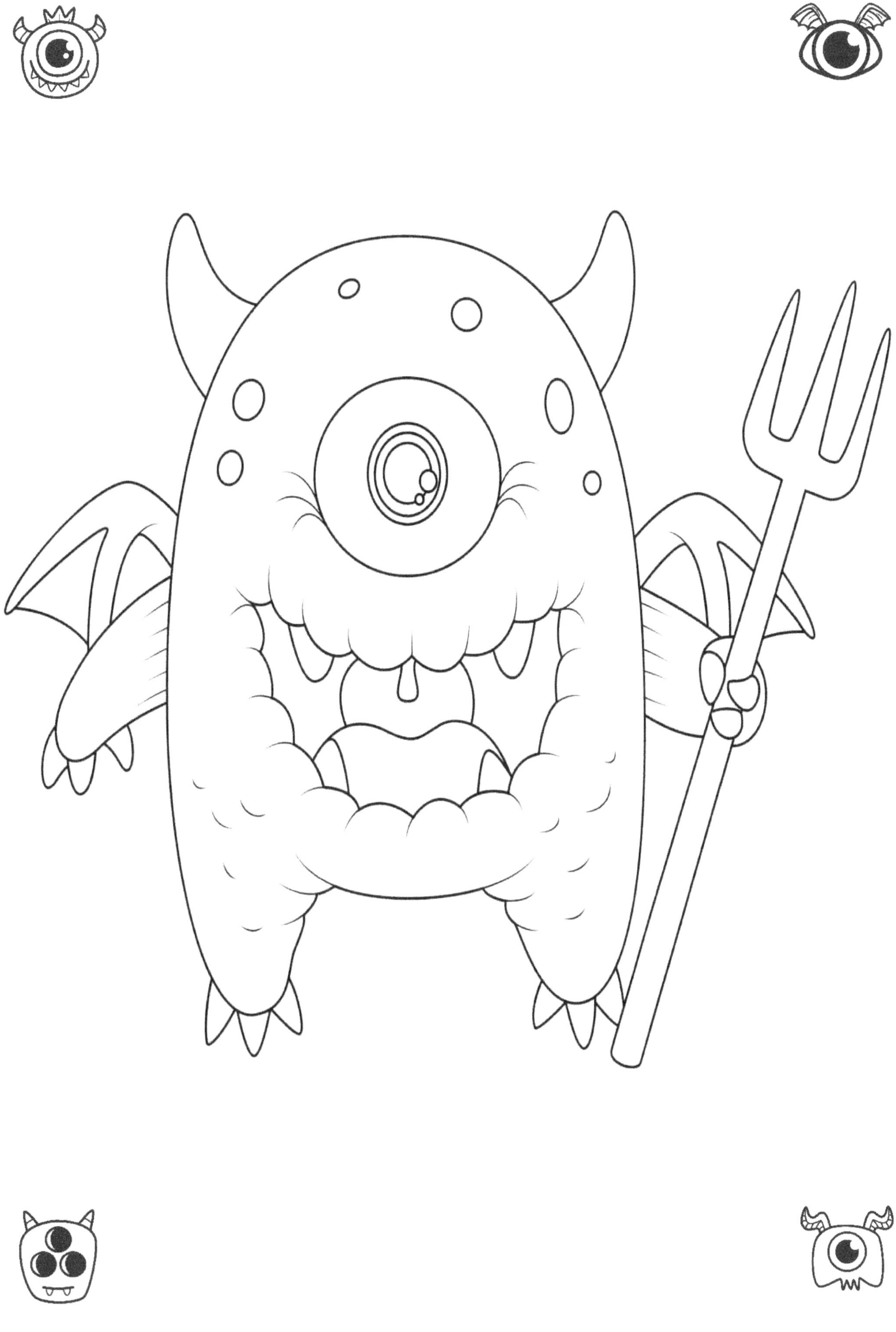

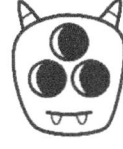
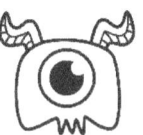

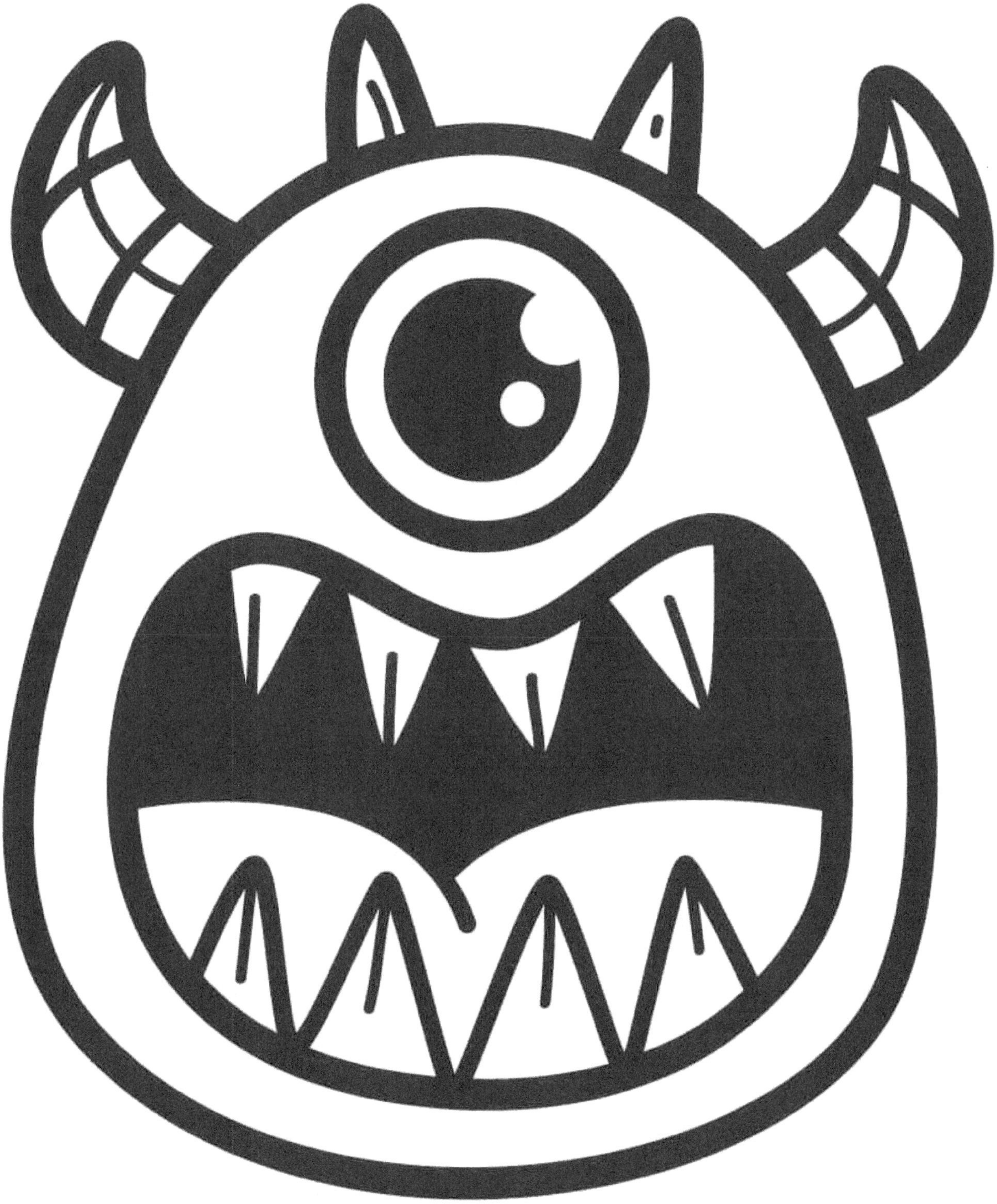

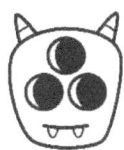
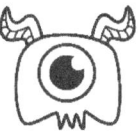

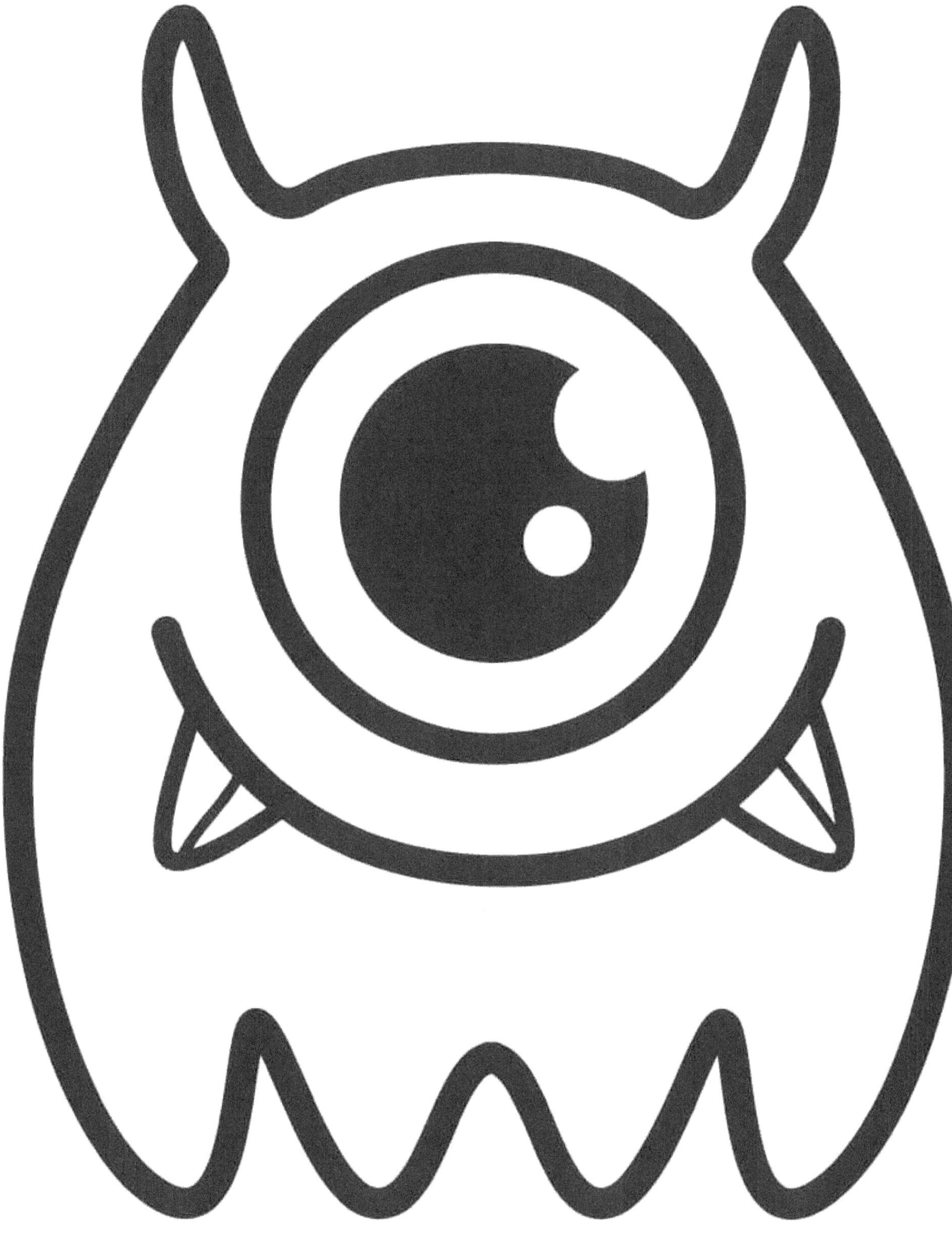

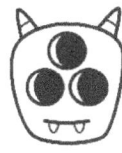
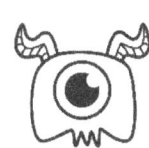

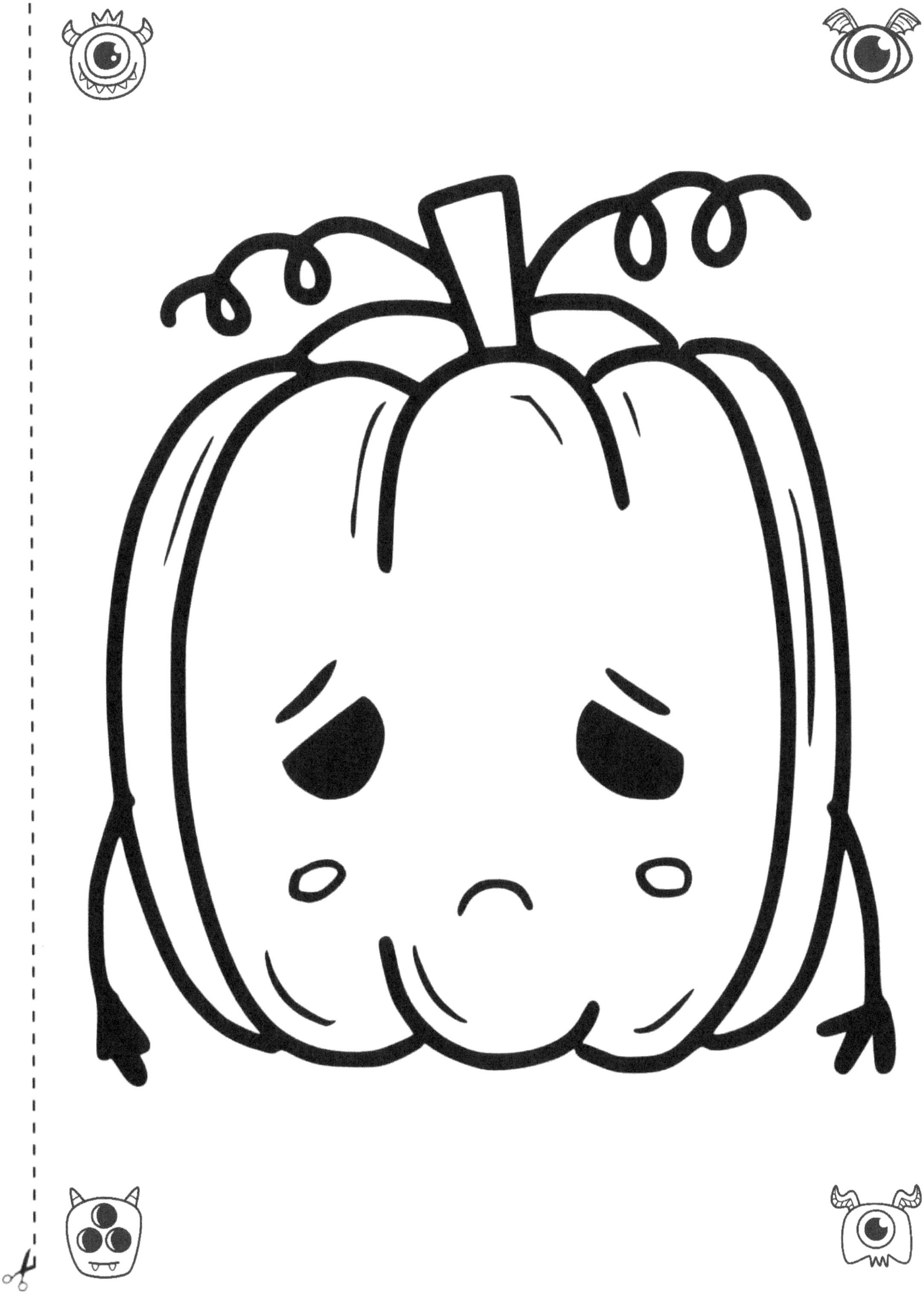

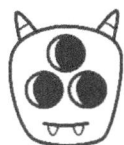
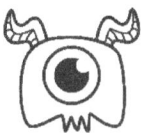

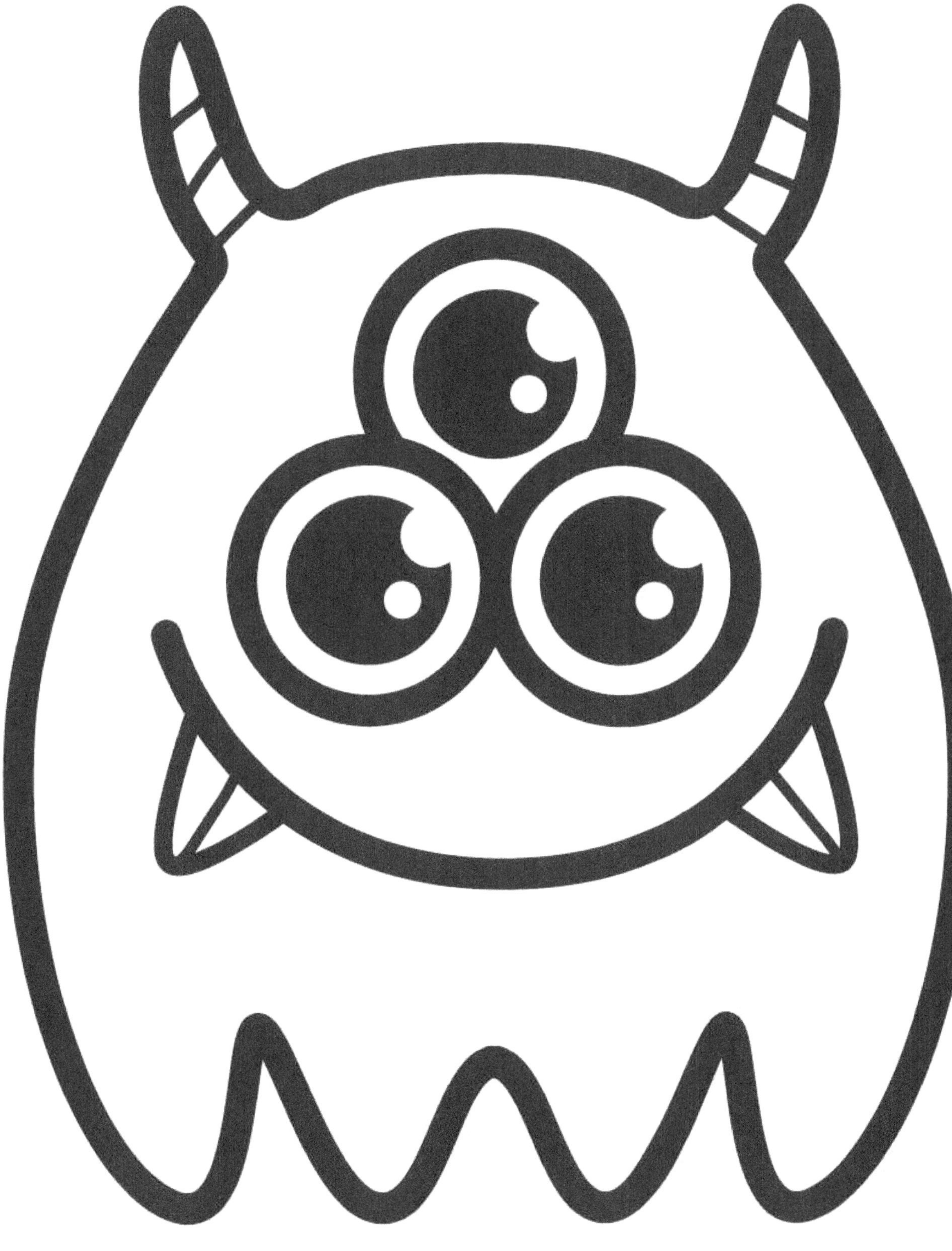

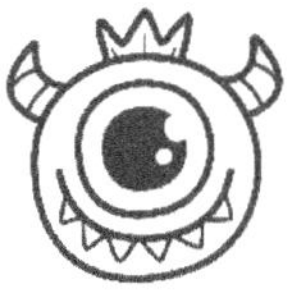

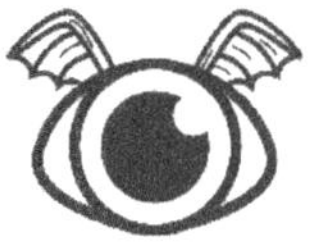

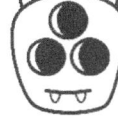
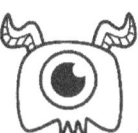

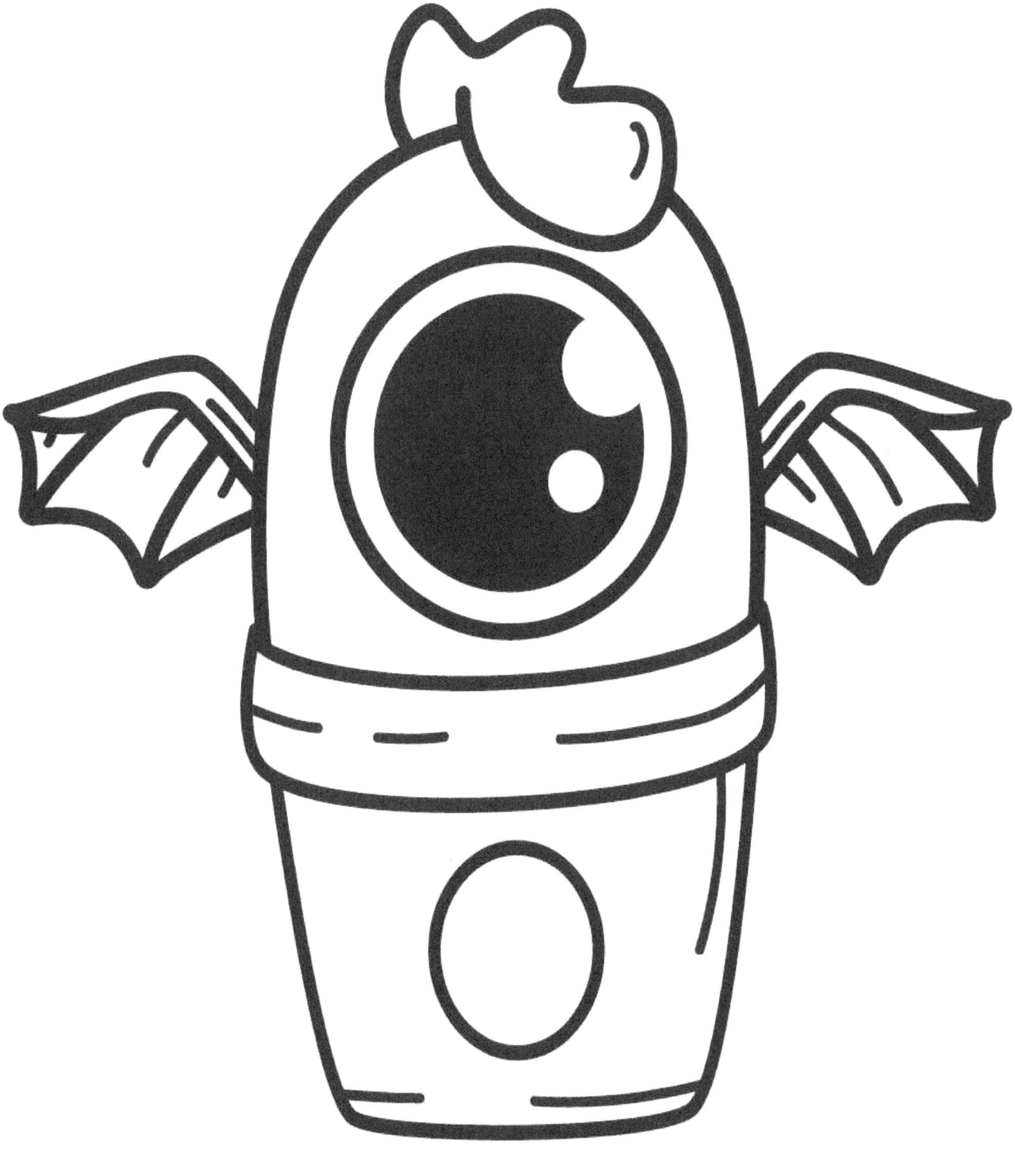

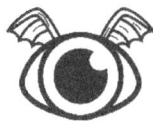
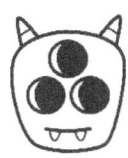
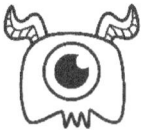

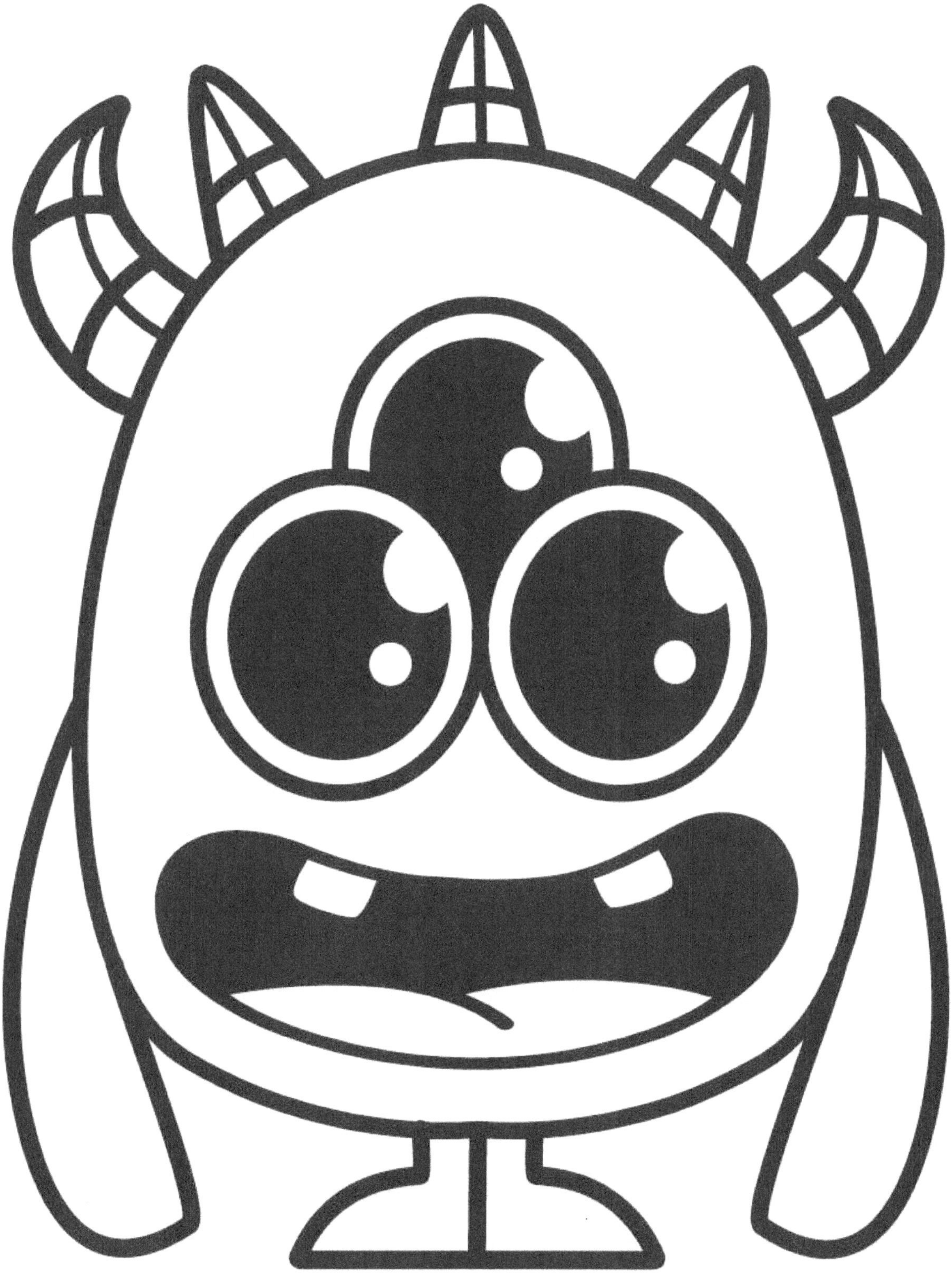

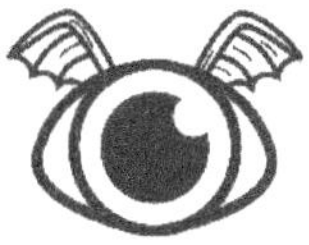

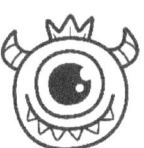

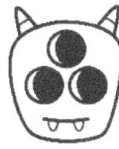
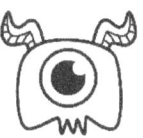

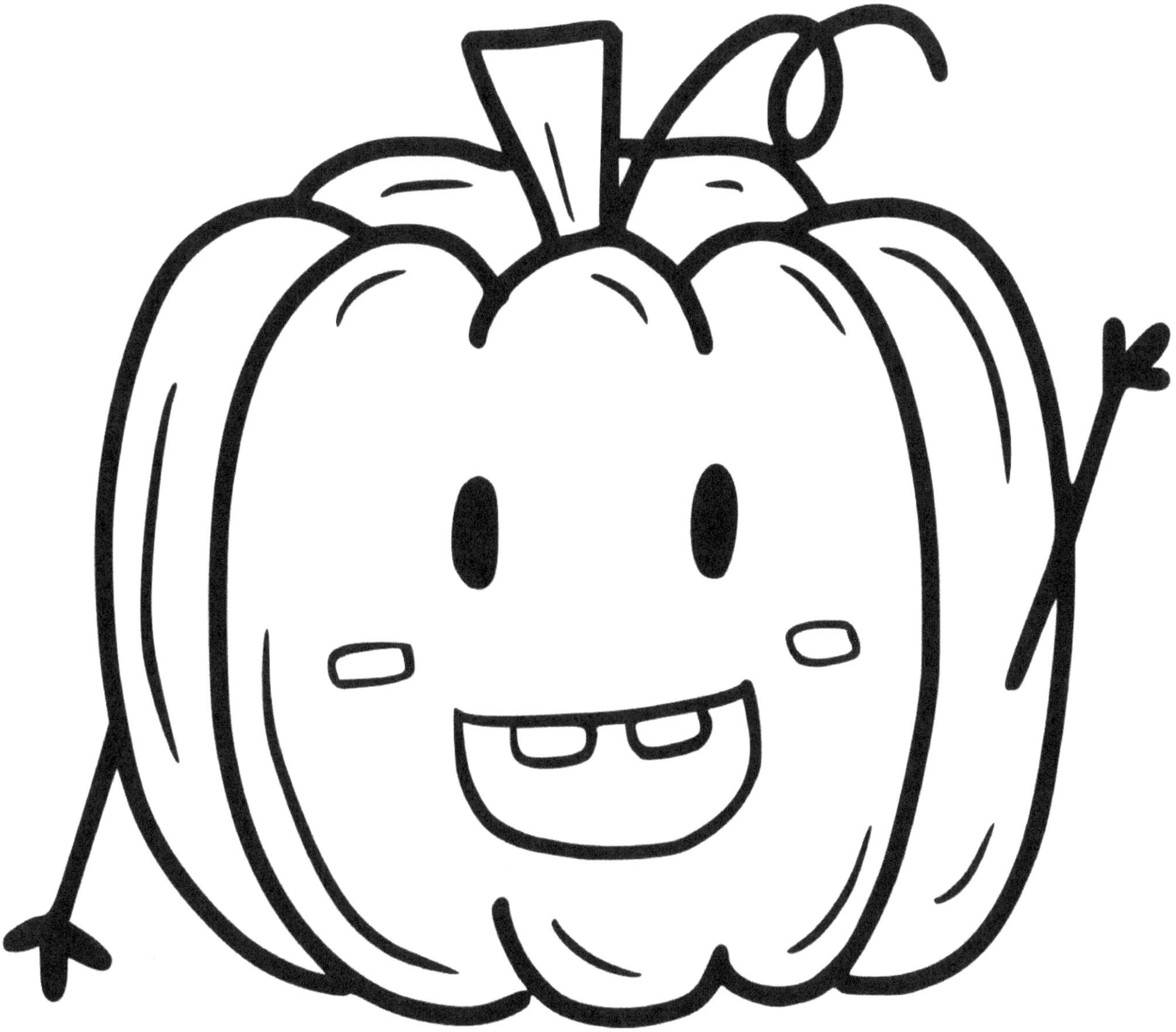

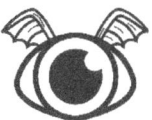
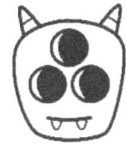
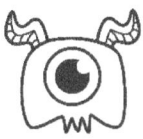

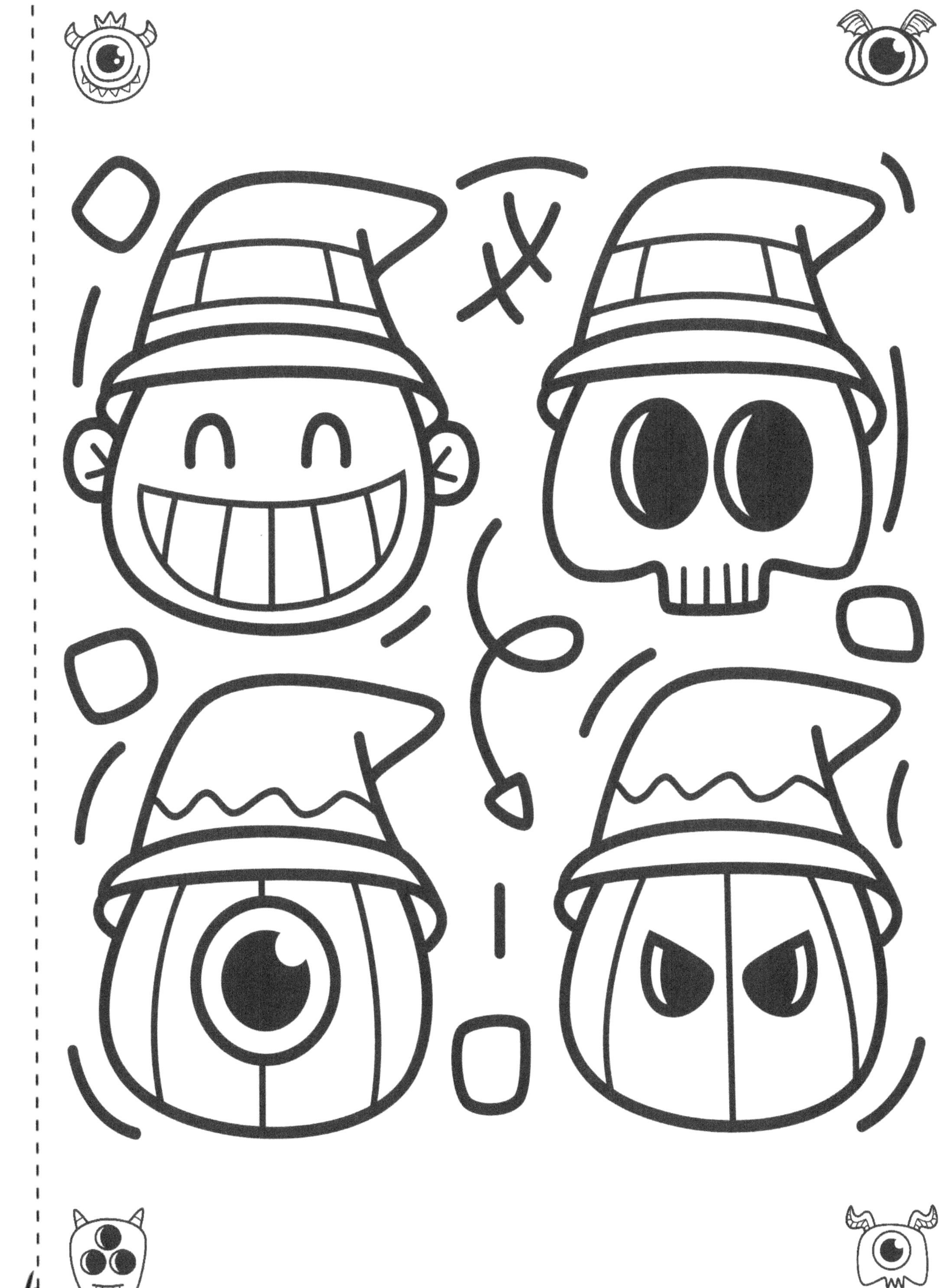

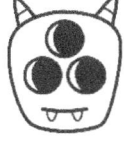
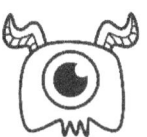

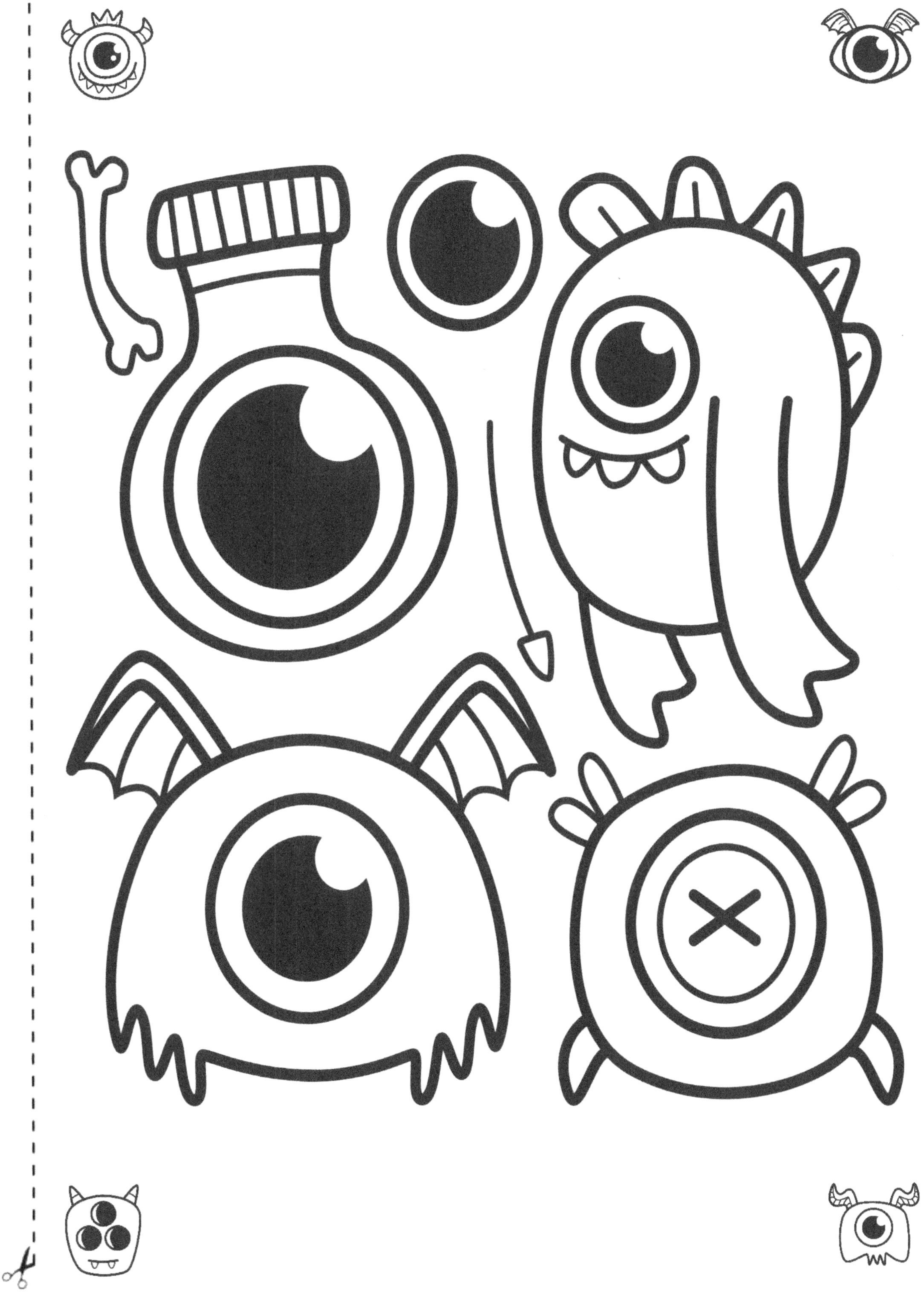

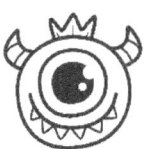
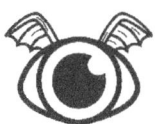
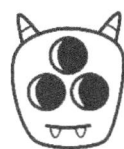
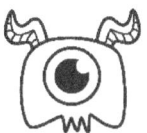

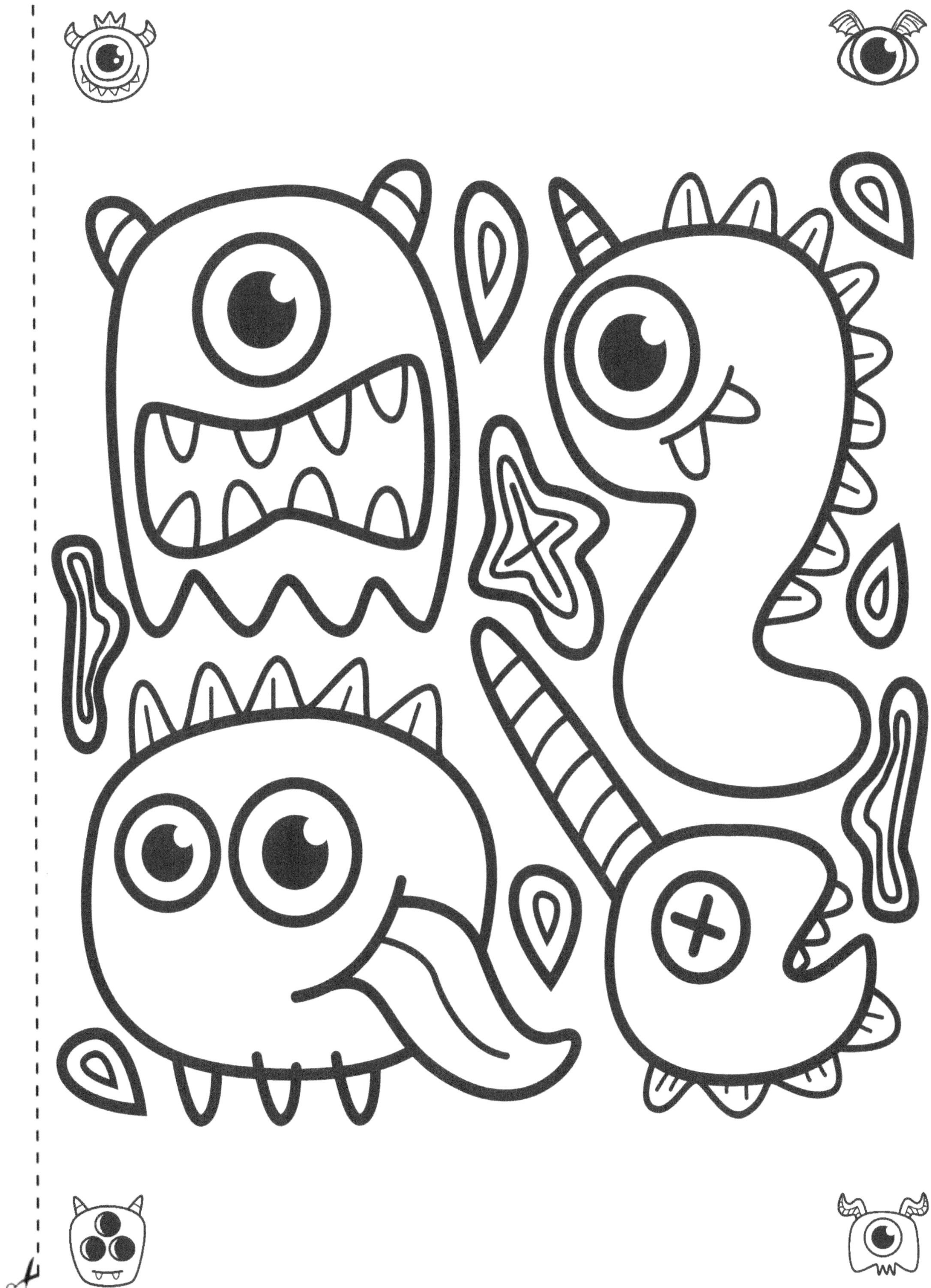

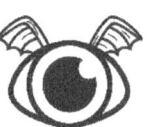
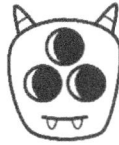
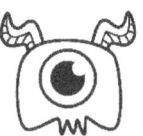

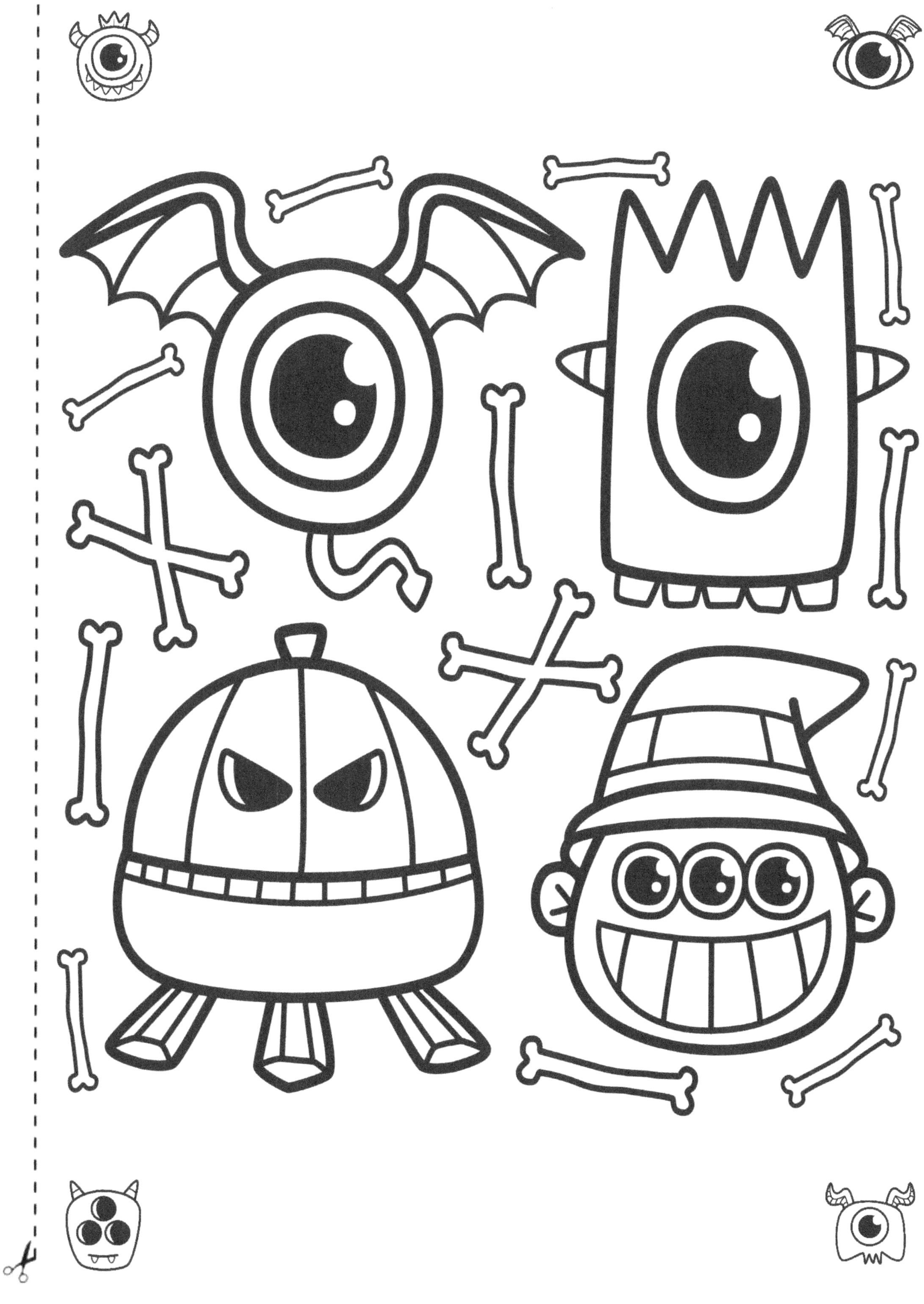

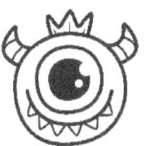
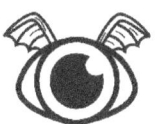
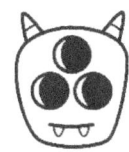
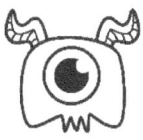

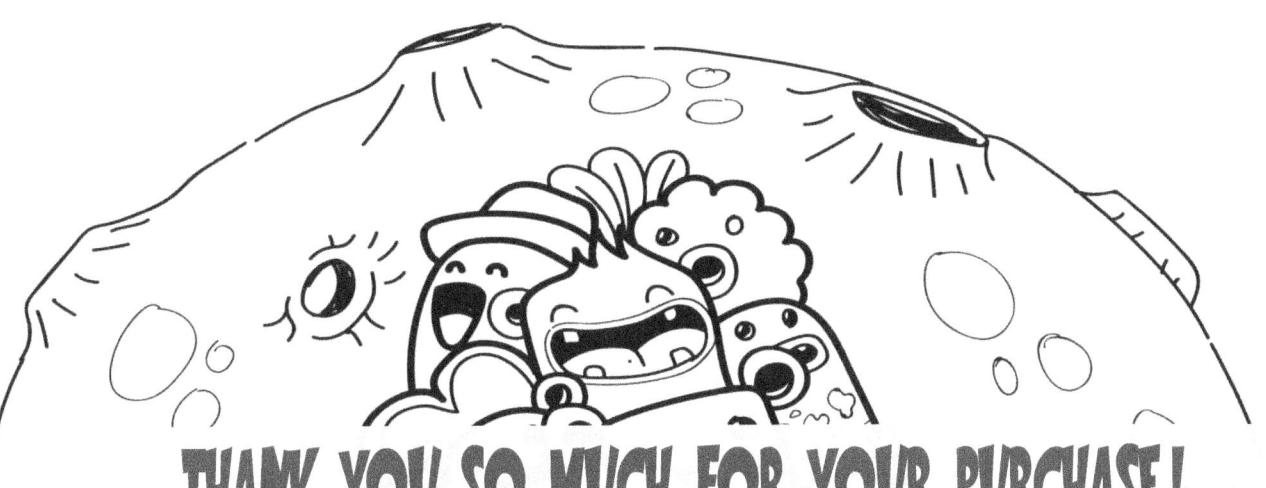

THANK YOU SO MUCH FOR YOUR PURCHASE!

IF YOU ENJOYED THIS BOOK, THEN PLEASE LEAVE AN AMAZON REVIEW. REVIEWS ARE THE LIFEBLOOD OF OUR PUBLISHING ENDEAVORS- LEAVING A POSITIVE REVIEW WOULD MEAN THE WORLD TO US.

THANKS AGAIN!

SOPHIE CAMPBELL
TFC GUIDE PUBLICATIONS

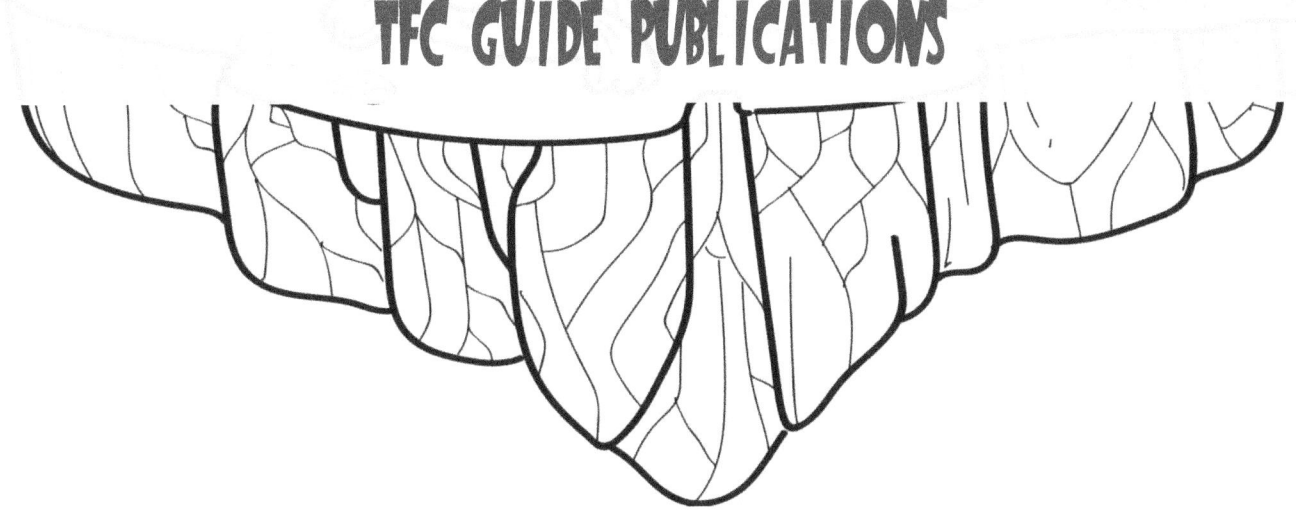

JUST A QUICK FAVOR...

PLEASE YOU FEEL FREE TO SEND US ANY COMMENT OR SUGGESTION THROUGH THE NEXT CHANNELS:

EMAIL: ADMIN@TFCGUIDE.COM

IF YOU LEAVE ME A REVIEW ON AMAZON ABOUT THIS BOOK, PLEASE WRITE ME AND I WILL SEND YOU DIGITAL TEMPLATES AS A GIFT.

OUR GOAL IS TO IMPROVE AND CREATE MORE VALUABLE BOOKS FOR YOU.
THANKS AGAIN!

SOPHIE CAMPBELL
TFC GUIDE PUBLICATIONS